A LIFETIME OF AWAKENINGS

CHRISTOPHER A. CLAXTON

BALBOA.
PRESS

A DIVISION OF HAY HOUSE

Balboa Press books may be ordered through booksellers or by contacting:

Balboa Press
A Division of Hay House
1663 Liberty Drive
Bloomington, IN 47403
www.balboapress.co.uk
1 (877) 407-4847

Because of the dynamic nature of the Internet, any web addresses or
links contained in this book may have changed since publication and
may no longer be valid. The views expressed in this work are solely those
of the author and do not necessarily reflect the views of the publisher,
and the publisher hereby disclaims any responsibility for them.

The author of this book does not dispense medical advice or prescribe the use
of any technique as a form of treatment for physical, emotional, or medical
problems without the advice of a physician, either directly or indirectly. The
intent of the author is only to offer information of a general nature to help
you in your quest for emotional and spiritual well-being. In the event you use
any of the information in this book for yourself, which is your constitutional
right, the author and the publisher assume no responsibility for your actions.

Any people depicted in stock imagery provided by Getty Images are
models, and such images are being used for illustrative purposes only.
Certain stock imagery © Getty Images.

Print information available on the last page.

ISBN: 978-1-9822-8029-1 (sc)
ISBN: 978-1-9822-8030-7 (e)

Balboa Press rev. date: 11/28/2018

Preface

"We are here to experience Human life and learn our lessons,
to do this we have to embrace change
as part of that journey.
We also have to learn to forgive, let go, and let life flow."

In carrying out my everyday work as a spiritual mentor I come across many people who are stuck in their lives, accepting situations that do not serve them, and living in a world of fear energy, afraid of taking that vital step for change.

A lot of these people turn to spirituality in an attempt to understand their problem and how they got there. Also they are in search of a way to make a step change for their lives and improve their situation for the better.

I can give sound advice and direction, as I do on a daily basis to these people, but what people have to understand is that all their solutions are held within themselves.

Your inner child, your soul, your spirit, call it what you wish, holds the keys to unlock any door that is put before you, and you are born with this knowing of who you are and what you are wanting on your very individual journey.

Acknowledge this inner child, live in your reality of the now, and do not let your thoughts and their fear of change bring your life to a halt.

In essence this book was written to show that no matter what life throws at you, it is possible to achieve the above once you remove any fear of change and just let life flow. From early years we have the feeling of self knocked out of us by society and its rules, by parents, and by the labelling we have placed upon us in the ever changing situations within our lives, causing us to lose the identity of self.

Society does not define you, your parents, your partners, your labels, do not define you. You are a wonderful, incredible being, on your own life journey, learning your own lessons as you go. Have your experiences, learn your lessons, do not fear change, it is an essential part of living and enjoying your journey. Embrace everything for what it is, it is your journey, your life, your experience, so listen to your inner child and live this life for you and nobody else.

Joy comes to those who go in search of it, do not be afraid to find your joy.

Acknowledgments

I would like to thank all the members of

The Wonderful World of Tarot & Spirituality
For their kindness, support, and generosity

Especially

Tony Lipscombe
Allen Tan
Karen Kay
Marie Fraser
Pat Sweeney
Gillian Dunn
Haidee Cabrera
Cecelia Cant
Ashlee Stephens
Donna Woomer
Annie Yeo
Jenni Tavenor
Kathy Furnley

I would also like to thank my editor
Bob Keenan

I especially have to thank my 3 beautiful Admin staff
for their total love, loyalty and support
throughout my journey.

Nichol Wong (Singapore)
Andrea Petratos (Australia)
Jen Keenan (U.S.A)

Blessings to all those people who played
their part in my life lessons.

A Little Understanding

Before detailing my life story and how I became to be the spiritual mentor I am today, I feel it is important to give some understandings and insights into what spirituality is about, what Tarot reading actually is, and what being an Empath entails. So that as you reach certain points within my story you have a clearer understanding of what I am referring to, especially for those who do not move in spiritual circles?

Like everything in this human life, the world of spirituality is a minefield of whom to put your trust in, who to believe, and who is talking rubbish in order to scam you out of money, unfortunately yes, that's the kind of world we live in. The worst part of spirituality is that it involves thousands perhaps millions of vulnerable people all around the world just looking for answers of a spiritual nature to what is happening in their lives. Out there and especially on the internet lurk many people who just want to prey upon and part these vulnerable people with their hard earned cash, seeing them as an easy target. So when searching around on the internet please be careful in who you place your trust.

Firstly let us take a look at this wonderful world of Tarot and its ups and downs.

I have been a spiritualist for the majority of my life, 69 years, and have done Tarot readings for almost 40 years, yet have never done it as a full time income generating source. I have always in any situation where I've charged for my services especially Tarot reading, tried to be honest and give the best value for money service that I can be, in addition to providing support, understanding and direction to my clients.

Why do I charge at all I can hear you ask? Well the answer is a simple one, and it all centres around energy. In my belief, I am spirit returned to Earth to have a human experience, therefore in order to exist within this human experience I must follow the human ways. Here on Earth the human way is that money is normally exchanged for human effort or energy and is needed in order to survive, so if I give you my time and my energy is it not therefore only right that you give me money representing your energy exchange? No different from all those who go to work on a daily basis to earn a living, as money is the essential human energy here to enable you to live your life. In addition, I've actually had to come to terms with the fact that humans have developed a certain train of thought, that if you don't charge for your services you are regarded as being sub standard or even having no value. What I provide within my service has immense value to my clients as the testimonials on my page will support.

There is also another down side of providing tarot readings free of charge which can be very detrimental to your health, and that is what is generally referred to in the spiritual community as "Energy Vampires". These are people usually with many life problems who have a total misunderstanding of what spirituality or Tarot reading can do for them, then because you don't charge, they feel they can just keep calling or messaging whenever they feel like it, day or night, and dump all their life problems on you as if you were their personal on call free psychologist. They have no care or understanding that this negative energy flow can totally drain or exhaust you. Nor do they care that you have your own life and its traumas to deal with, because it's free they feel they have permanent access to you, and so charging for your service definitely deters these vampires.

A lot of people have misconceptions around Tarot, thinking that the purpose of a reading is to predict a given future, but the reality is nothing of the sort.

In life, nothing is written in stone. Life is a flowing thing that can change from moment to moment, or in the blink of an eye, therefore nothing can be predicted via a Tarot reading. What tarot mysteriously does, and even I can't explain it after almost 40 years of doing it, is put you in contact with your client's life, where they are in their NOW, this moment in time in their life. It can also give the reader an insight to how they got there from the cards that are drawn. Once the reader connects with this moment they can advise as to where the possible paths may lead providing nothing changes, thus giving some insight for the client.

Understand that the 78 pictorial cards that make up a Tarot deck are just a representation in picture form of the stages in life, the journey we all make.

It is a journey that has been trodden by billions of previous humans, and your journey is actually no different to any that has been trodden before and your outcome on the path your treading at this moment has a predictable outcome providing nothing changes.

When I read for you I connect with your now, your present moment and situation, and so my reading is based on where I find you in your current life which in turn leads to all its possible outcomes. However, if tomorrow you take some action or make some change because of the free will you were born with, or even if somebody within your close environment takes some action, the whole outcome could change. So how can anything be written in stone? Because the possibility of change lurks around every corner, be it by choice or enforced.

A good tarot reader is closer to a psychologist than anybody would give them credit for. They are a support and advice service and most people come to them seeking that support and advice to help them see a way forward usually from a difficult or unhappy situation. We have to be open and honest with them and council them as best we can within our knowledge and capability, and so life experience can come in very handy. All that said, this is the definition and description of a normal Tarot reader and does not take into account the "Intuitive" readers which are a whole new ball game altogether, bringing medium abilities in to play. Plus there is still the question of who guides you to pick the relevant cards in the first place? Is it chance or are we actually guided to certain cards? However, that is a discussion for another time, all I can say is that genuine Tarot readers are not fortune tellers, they do not predict the future. The whole purpose behind me doing readings or any spiritual work is to help people in times of need or distress and provide guidance and support. My spiritual journey has never been about earning an income or extra money, although at times it is necessary in order to obtain the tools to continue my work, and my motto has always been to help people to help themselves.

Now I take you into an explanation and understanding of what spiritualism is actually all about. It is nothing new. In fact although the history books will tell you that it started in the U.S.A in the 1850's, yet the basic understanding of spiritual beliefs have been around for a long time, and some of its teachings can be traced back to Ancient Greece. A lot of modern day spiritual thinking has its roots firmly based in Greek Mythology and their thinking, although adapted to suit over the years.

The fact is the whole of spiritualism is based around self help, using and developing your own thought processes and changing the way you see things, therefore the things you see change, it is all about perception.

In order to get to grips with the deeper understanding of spiritualism and where it is derived from, you first have to get your heads around energy, because that is exactly what we all are, little individual balls of energy, surrounded by lots of other forms of energy, all interacting with each other in some way. Next, take on the scientifically proved theory that energy cannot die but can be transmuted into a different form or being of existence. This is not fiction, but fact.

Following that thread of thought and knowledge, all energy comes from a single source, and therefore all living things are just a fragment of that original source that has broken off, and because we as humans have to label everything we call that source God. As humans, we like to give names and labels to everything so that we can recognise what it is, what it should do, where it should be, or how it should behave. It is actually irrelevant what religious belief you have, or what label your belief places upon this source, because in the end all the labels, and all the religions, lead back to the same source, to the same point of creation.

Each religion has its own stories to tell, its own values to impose, but amongst spiritualists it is generally accepted that we are all connected and are all the same, all coming from the same source energy. Even if we look different or speak a different language, every living thing has come from the same source energy and therefore all start at the same place, and probably all end up back in the same place.

So the million dollar question is, "what happens when we die?"

In fact we don't die, as energy cannot die. This human shell that carries this ball of energy around may cease to function anymore because it is time limited.

The energy, the spirit, the soul, call it what you like, cannot die, and therefore must go somewhere else. All the above are scientifically known facts and not pie in the sky theories. They are the reality of energy and its existence.

From that understanding we can begin to accept the premise of "a spirit" as being a ball of energy that has left its defunct human body, therefore in turn is existing somewhere else, either transmuted into another form, or has returned to its original source.

We again as humans label that place of the original source as "Heaven" others have given it many names over the centuries and based on their own belief systems.

The other known fact is that different energy sources can react or interact with another energy source, therefore making it quite plausible that if two energy sources meet that they can communicate with each other, as long as they vibrate on the same level.

Why do people find it difficult to accept the concept that some people can connect and interact with spirit?

All you have to do to understand how it works is to imagine yourself like a radio, when it's switched off you get nothing, no sound. When you switch it on add electricity to it wonderful things begin to happen. All of a sudden these energy waves we couldn't see hits the radio receiver and produces the sound, and we accept that without questioning it. Spirit connection is just the same.

Communicating with the spirit world is similar, if you as a receiver are tuned in to the right frequency or vibration then you can communicate. You can communicate with them, and they can communicate with you. But if you are not plugged in, turned on, or tuned in, you will receive nothing. And if you stay turned on and tuned in communication can flow to you at any time. This is what we call spiritual intuition. I am really going to leave the mechanics of spiritualism there and just talk about living as a spiritualist and what that means.

The dictionary meaning of spiritualist is "Somebody who believes in the existence of, and ability to communicate with spirit." However, there is also a way of living as a spiritualist, and that is synonymous with being a person whose highest priority is to be loving to both themselves and others and to be conscious of our connection and oneness to all living things. We are all from one energy source and should respect that. This is my explanation on spiritualism and the source of all my beliefs, which have been developed over my life time through various situations and experiences.

I now just need you to understand the last situation, the basic meaning of what being an Empath is, so that it is clear when you come across it in my story.

We have to first step back into the understanding that energy sources can react with each other, and then understand that emotions, feelings, and thoughts, are all a form of vibrational energy. With that accepted, then the main problem with being an Empath is that you are liable to absorb other people's emotions, thoughts and feelings. You can become highly attuned to other people's moods, feeling everything about this neighbouring energy and it can be extreme especially if that energy is in a negative form such as anger or anxiety.

It can also be very draining of your own energy levels as energy feeds off energy, and can leave you feeling very lethargic when confronted by it.

With all this outline information and understanding in place, we can now move into my story, which is literally the whole story of my life from birth to this present moment.

It reveals all the highs and lows, human and spiritual experiences, and people who have been catalysts in my life and helped me to gain my own consciousness.

It is a patchwork of things that have brought me to become the spiritual mentor I am today, and given me so much understanding of human life.

"The Now"

As a modern day spiritualist and spiritual mentor, I come across many people who have had an experience of awakening in all sorts of different ways, ranging from the overnight light bulb moment to those grappling around in the dark trying to find an understanding of what is happening to them and why? I have also come across many situations in between. For some reason they have been inexplicably drawn to the spiritual world and start searching for answers. Usually all awakenings are triggered by a difficult human situation or traumatic incident which they find hard to reason with or understand. Some are drawn through grief, the loss of a loved one or even through a near death experience, where the person involved have lived through the experience of dying and then being drawn back having been to the other side of life. So, however they have experienced their awakening, it often leads them to turn to the unconventional or other belief systems in search of some kind of explanation for the thoughts and emotions they are feeling, which in turn quite often leads them to spirituality to look for the answers and understanding.

My awakening, however, was slow to develop and happened over a lifetime of experiences, not a single light bulb moment, but through various events both human and spiritual that brought me closer to my consciousness and spiritual beliefs and understanding of life and eventually to the person I am today.

For me, it has been a very long hard road with many life lessons thrown in my path, and I now sit in retrospect able to see how everything has brought me to my now.

I have no regrets or remorse for anything that happened to me or all the lessons I had to learn in order to reach this spiritual understanding of life. After all, as they say, "we are just spirit having a human experience" and so we are here to have this full blown human experience, and everything that this entails.

The internet is full of thousands of video's and explanations about the processes of the spiritual awakening, but what is one person's spiritual awakening can be totally different to another's, because of where they are in their life and what triggered it.

As there is no "one size fits all" solution or explanation for a spiritual awakening, people can still remain just as confused and bewildered after watching many people's explanations, and will actually just need gentle understanding support.

There are in fact no clear guidelines or defined patterns to an individual personal awakening, because it is just that. It is personal and individual, and arrived at through their own life experience, which can be one of many.

Sometimes human experiences or traumas cause us to look deep within our souls and make us start to look for answers of a spiritual nature, and this may be the first time they have ever thought about spirituality.

For some this can even be linked to, or relate to their religious upbringing and belief systems that have been imposed on them, which now clash with how they are feeling or seeing something, just like you will see how similarly all my different experiences made me challenge my beliefs and understandings.

For others, it can be what we called during the hippy period of the 60's, "The Searching for the Meaning of Life" just looking for a purpose and understanding of why we are here, and trying to make sense of it.

This was triggered on occasions by the use of drugs at that time, especially the use of psychedelic drugs like L.S.D, which altered the state of mind and also gave people out of body experiences, a subject all on its own. Some people talk of vivid dreams in which God or Jesus spoke to them and they would describe this experience as a religious calling, and so go on their path of religious discovery trying to find a reason for their vision.

So we now see awakenings can come in various guises and through various life experiences, but there is one thing we cannot doubt, awakenings exist, and are becoming more and more commonplace in the world. Every week thousands more people turn to spirituality, looking for some kind of answer or understanding.

As the world creates more and more unanswered questions and difficult situations people start to challenge the deeper meaning of life and its purpose.

During my lifetime I have seen the growth in spiritualism, and the changing views within society towards it as a belief system, and there is now more acceptance of it, with some spiritual mentors becoming like celebrities in their own right.

Obviously, this has all been aided and helped through the creation and expansion of the internet, which puts the world and all the information contained in it at your fingertips. Unfortunately, not all things found on the internet are for the best. It has also created a breed of people who see it as a way of making an income through preying on the vulnerability of others, which really gets me annoyed having to watch the beauty of spirituality being misused and abused in this way, and displaying the worse aspects of human nature.

In my case, and the point behind my very personal life story, is to show that we can have a lifetime of little awakenings, which all joined together get us to arrive at our final consciousness and spiritual understanding. Through having a variety or mixture of human experiences and then making sense of them on a spiritual level they have brought me to a massive final awakening which led me to become a spiritual mentor and pass my knowledge on. This collection of experiences has brought me to my own personal truths, my own personal understanding of my "I AM", that spirit within, my soul, and my spiritual understanding of life, or as some would say "seeing the light".

Strangely enough I'm going to start my story from the NOW, who I am now, where I am now, plus the understanding I have in connection to the spiritual world, and the personal truths I arrived at, all my little awakenings as I call them.

At the time of writing this I have just passed through my 69th birthday so I'm no youngster by any means, although people say I look nothing like my age, plus even within myself I only feel and behave like a 40 year old. Maybe spirituality also keeps us young? A point also to note, and very importantly, is that I have never read a complete book in my life, in fact, I doubt that I have ever picked up more than a handful of books during my whole 69 years. This means that I have never studied spirituality in any depth from any source, so my understanding and beliefs are not from some regurgitated book knowledge or learning, it is all purely from my life experiences and spiritual encounters, and how they have impacted my life, and brought me to my own personal spiritual understanding.

If you couple the life experiences with this very deep rooted knowing of spiritual matters for which I have no concrete provable understanding of where all this knowing comes from it makes the whole awakening a massive thing.

Sometimes it feels like I was born with this encyclopaedia of spiritual knowledge printed and held somewhere deep inside me. Quite often I can start talking about spiritual matters and words just come out of my mouth like somebody else is speaking, and it often leaves me saying "where did that come from?" Or sometimes I start to write pieces for my group page, and my fingers just have a mind of their own, which feels like I am somebody's secretary with this person dictating and I am just typing what they say, which can be explained as a type of auto writing.

I only have theories behind this knowing of spiritual knowledge which have been arrived at through examining certain coincidences and happenings in my life and comparing my experience with others. In the end, all of this has culminated in what I refer to as "my awakenings", this constant drip feeding of spiritual awareness that has gone on all through my life.

My now finds me the owner of a spiritual page called "The Wonderful World of Tarot and Spirituality" which originally was just "The wonderful world of Tarot" and you will see when the change came about as you read on.

Currently we have two thousand six hundred followers or members at various stages of their spiritual development or understanding of where they are, and all are seeking answers of some kind and with a lot of them just requiring support on their confusing spiritual journey. I currently have 3 wonderful admin staff who really are angels in their own right, and who support me with everything I do.

My admin staff create a wonderful caring family atmosphere on the page supporting people wherever they can and because they are from different countries in the world the page gets 24/7 support. One of them, Jen, who herself came to us after her near death experience, is also determined to make a dream of mine come true around reading and lecturing around the world, and she is already organising the start of the tour in the USA next year, as over half our members are from there.

Although it started off as a purely Tarot card teaching page in April 2017, it very quickly changed direction after a couple of months, through the chance meeting of a very special person who since has encouraged me to share a lot of my spiritual knowledge and understanding, and in turn it has transformed the page and she has been my guide and inspiration to do this work ever since.

Even the conception of the page has its own mysterious beginnings which to me in retrospect is also proof of guides at work pushing me in the direction of my life purpose and reason for this incarnation. Even though up to this moment my final life purpose has not yet been revealed in full, I believe all the pieces are being put into place all the time until the divine timing is right to do what I was sent here for.

My spiritual page came about after knowing a lovely woman called Kelsey for over 5 years, who I met and chatted with on a fairly regular basis on the Internet.

She is a single mum who gave up her nursing career to look after one of her sons when he became ill and needed ongoing personal care and we became friends exchanging our daily lives and chatting about anything and everything as you do, and often discussing her new men friends who were giving her attention.

She only lived 10 miles from me and I often threatened her with the scary idea of meeting up for coffee one day, but the strange thing is that we have never met during the whole 5 years of our friendship for some unknown reason.

As a believer in that we meet everybody for a reason in this life, I often wondered why we met, what our purpose in meeting was. She was fully aware that I read Tarot, and I used to consult the cards for her occasionally to help give her some guidance especially around relationships, but never once had she actually asked me to read for her or take advantage through our friendship which I greatly respected. Many people would just abuse this kind of friendship.

One night we were discussing Tarot and she said "why didn't I start a face book page teaching Tarot because you're very good at what you do and people could learn and benefit from your understanding and knowledge." To cut a long story short, several hours later I was on the computer with not a clue how to do it, but I spent the whole of the next 3 days and nights working things out and putting the whole page together ready for launch.

I was feeling very motivated and full of energy using skills I didn't even know I possessed and I had little sleep and even less thought for food as I ploughed on getting it ready like a man possessed.

So if I was to acknowledge what a real catalyst was, a word we commonly use in Tarot reading, then Kelsey was that catalyst who arrived or was brought before me in order to drive me forward on my spiritual path. It was also a very big awakening that I still had something to offer the world which I'd never even thought of until then and then heaven has a strange way of getting you to do essential stuff.

It was like how we describe the meaning of the 2 of Wands in our decks, "taking that first step of a thousand mile journey, not knowing where it will take you."

Little was I to know from that inception just how things would change in my life, and I couldn't have imagined how this page I created would eventually have such an impact on people's lives. The page turned into something completely different from what it was put together for, and took a much deeper spiritual path which attracted people although retaining its original Tarot teaching and roots.

Tarot is just a reflection of life and its journey, a journey trodden billions of times before, with nothing new to experience that hasn't already been experienced.

The page was gaining momentum, and within a couple of weeks, I had appointed 4 people as the initial admin of the page to help with the day to day running as we already had a few hundred demanding members so it was becoming quite busy. Everything was moving forward at great speed and during the initial month I became very attracted to one admin in particular who gave me a lot of attention and we became very close friends very quickly and attracted to each other on a very human level.

She was from a totally different world to me being some 30 years younger, she was Muslim, married with a child, and living in the USA, in fact all the reasons why in a human world we should not let this get too serious because of all the problems we would encounter. For some strange reason I never really noticed the difficulty in any of this, I was attracted to her and we had spirituality in common, so there was always something to discuss besides just everyday life and what was happening on the page.

Within a few weeks she started talking about the Twin Flame connection which I was really not up to speed with in the modern spiritual world, so she explained it to me and all the theoretical journeys of the twin flame connection and everything she said resonated as being a possibility.

The only knowledge I had around this subject was some knowing buried deep within based around Ancient Greek mythology and what happens at our creation.

The Ancient Greeks believed that at our point of creation a single spark divided into two parts, one female, one male, which then separated and went their separate ways. From that moment on and to put it simply, their purpose and driving force was then to find each other again so that their spirit could reunite in order to become whole. Once achieved, they could return to their heaven and remain there in an elevated position amongst the Gods. Failure to find your missing half in this lifetime would mean reincarnating time after time until eventually you found your missing piece, and achieved wholeness. So the ancient Greek version was a similar story on the same lines of the modern twin flame theory, but without some of the additional stages that have been added over the years in the modern version. Like most stories based in religions or beliefs they have been added to or changed over the centuries to suit its followers. I could see the connection to what she was saying, even if not totally convinced by the modern theory and modern interpretation of the stages of the process.

Although our relationship was fun on a very human level, which was something that had been missing from my life for quite a few years since my divorce, she was more involved with esoteric aspects of spiritualism and fighting darkness and entities.

Her spirituality was directed more at dealing and fighting the dark forces and entities in the world also her mission to free all Muslim women from their bondage, with the latter being something I admired in her. I on the other hand possess a spiritualism that is more about self help, sharing, and supporting people through their journey. My spiritualism has a gentle and loving feel to it, and so our spiritualism comes from different places, and so cracks started to form in our relationship as we argued more and more.

The Real Twin Flame Arrives.........

Some two and a half months into the page new members were joining at a rate of anything up to 100 a week, and one day I was checking through the list of people who had joined the group during the night before whilst I was sleeping.

As I went through them, I was strangely attracted to one member in particular who although I didn't know at the time, was soon to have a massive impact upon my life from that moment on, and also that of the page, and direction it would take.

I took one look at her picture and the connection was just instantaneous, I wanted to know everything about her. On a much deeper level, there was this incredible feeling of total connectedness, it was like a coming home, as if I had known her all my life and yet had been apart from her for ages. I knew nothing about her, except that which was obvious from her picture, that she was Asian, possibly Chinese and obviously younger than me. I couldn't wait to send her a message and get to know why I had all these incredible feelings going on and the only thing I could think of saying in my message was "not sure of our time difference?" Then hoping and praying that she would reply.

I really was in a state of excitement and confusion over my emotions and just how much I was being drawn to her. There was this massive feeling of relief when she replied, like I had found something that I had earlier lost that was so important to me and now I had found it again.

What I wasn't aware of at that moment was that in fact there was a similar situation going on in her mind which I was very quickly to discover as we started talking.

After some discussion through messaging each other, I found out yet again that there were these massive differences between us, she was Asian and of Chinese decent, 24 years younger than me, married with children, and lived eight thousand miles away in Singapore. I felt this massive awakening happening, this knowing, this instant outpouring

11

of love, as if my whole life had been in preparation for this moment of meeting, and that she was sent to complete me and be a major part of my future spiritual path. The meeting with my real twin flame.

At this point I don't want to go into too much detail about this beautiful relationship. Because as I write this, it has not yet reached any point that I can describe as a conclusion. Everything is still up in the air, but once this story reaches its own conclusion, I will write a whole book based purely upon my real life twin flame experience so that people can compare it to all the theories already written. As we have got to know each other over the past 15 months, I have found in her a peace and a connectedness that I had never felt with another person. After some research on the Internet, I got to understand about fake twin flames, something new again which I had no awareness of previously, and the purpose of a fake twin flame in preparing you for the meeting with your real twin.

Because of this new found understanding, and the constant arguing around spiritualism, the original relationship with the first admin, my fake twin, came to its natural end.

So yes, another awakening, another real life spiritual experience, but this time to the reality of an incredible spiritual love, a coming home after being in the wilderness all my life, plus the existence and modern understanding of twin flames in both their forms.

Through this coming together and this new connection with my twin flame I found energy, drive, inspiration, and purpose. It was like a light switch turning on, and writings just flowed out of me and onto the page, another catalyst in my life who was to be the torch holder for my spiritual journey.

Even now I am not sure what is happening, but I can consciously feel my guides pushing and pushing me forward like I have no resistance to it. Not only the writings, but even the readings I was doing became different, so much more intuitive and so much more accurate and filled with a much more loving and caring feel to them, it is like my twin flame has opened up every aspect of my spiritual being, and now couldn't imagine a single day without her by my side to encourage me.

Even though I have read Tarot for almost 40 years, even I could feel a difference in the content and delivery of my readings, and the 5 star reviews from paid readings started flowing in on my private page.

I don't take on too many private readings at the moment as I am very time restricted with all the work on the page and the regular weekend lives I do. My twin has been my inspiration for just about everything I have written or done within the group.

Since meeting her and our coming together, she has been the catalyst for me to become the person I am today, able to communicate my spirituality more effectively.

On our page we have an active on line Tarot course, live readings, live guided meditations, our own spiritual goods shop, an "In conversation" live where people can ask questions around anything spiritual in addition to the many spiritual posts I write. I am currently putting together some videos aimed at spiritual mentoring for my group and also discussing a You Tube channel to reach a wider audience.

There is just so much happening, and I am so busy, all because of my twin flames inspiration and belief in me. I can have as many as 1500 people at my weekend live readings and the live guided meditations are becoming very popular. I do love the personal touch of my page and that people can talk to me either in our 24/7 family chat or personally, which also makes it different from many other internet pages.

My twin and I have also discovered other connections, which are far more spiritual or esoteric in nature. After only a few weeks of knowing my twin flame I woke one morning to discover that one of my original admin had secretly started her own page and was inviting people from my group to join her, including other admin.

Yes, who was it that discovered what was going on but my new twin flame. She jumped in fearlessly to condemn them for their deceitful actions engaging in an open verbal battle in our groups chat box.

During the verbal exchange that followed I sat and watched her defending and protecting me like a guardian angel, a crusader fighting for the light, fighting for justice. My vision was of her wearing golden armour wielding her sword relentlessly as she waded in to protect her twin. She really was an angelic figure in my vision.

Later in a private conversation we had, she also mentioned about putting on her armour and going to battle for justice, before I could even mention my vision. Needless to say, I was hurt at the betrayal of people I had trusted, and it took me some days to get over it, at the same time the connection between me and my new twin flame became even stronger and I gained even more strength knowing she was by my side. It really felt like she had been sent to guide, motivate, and protect me, to ensure I took up my spiritual path.

On another occasion, I had a very vivid dream one night in which I met an old bearded Chinese man dressed in ragged clothes wearing sandals on his feet, a very gentle and humble man. He led me to a garden which was quite orderly and very beautiful and peaceful, where sat a young Chinese boy who was whittling wooden dragon figures from wood. The old man handed me two of the boys dragons as a gift, with not a word spoken, just a smile on his face and a recognition of each other that passed between us, a feeling not like two strangers meeting for the first time, but like we had met at some point previously. There was this knowing between us.

This dream was so real, so vivid and seemed to have gone on for ages, it felt like he had handed me my Chinese twin flame in the form of this wooden dragon and he was giving me his blessing, though we both still speculate and have not worked out what the second dragon symbolised.

The next morning I told her of my dream and she asked me to describe him, which I did in detail, including the garden we walked in which was calm and beautiful. With a certain shock that I had met him, she told me that I had described her guide down to the last detail.

My twin possessed a personal belief that her guide was Lao Tzu the famous Chinese writer, spiritualist, and philosopher, who compiled and wrote the teachings of the Tao Te Ching, much loved and written about by the late great Dr Wayne Dyer in his book "Change your thoughts, change your life," which was sent me as a gift but I have yet to find time to read.

She had also received confirmation of Lao Tzu's existence as her guide from several Chinese mediums she has had consultations with over time.

I have met this spiritual being on 3 different occasions in dreams or in meditation, and each time there is this incredible connected and familiar feeling.

There is this emotion that goes on inside me that we have met before, which I can't possibly begin to explain in understandable human terms, as these visions and the recognition is so real he feels like a part of me in some way. I get a feeling of meeting somebody who I have known in a previous life, who I've been connected to.

I have this very esoteric feeling and connection to my twin flames guide, I also seem to already know all of his teachings and sayings as if they were my own, and it's a very weird feeling to instinctively know all this when I have never read a book in my life. Neither have I ever watched anything anywhere on Lao Tzu's teachings until I met my twin flame. All I can understand about this connection is that it came alive through meeting my twin flame. Almost all my spiritual learning has happened slowly over my whole life, through the different people I have met and the experiences I have had, so how could I know all this stuff from Lao Tzu? I had never even heard his name before, so I leave that for you to fathom out and hopefully for me to discover one day in some moment of enlightenment.

Being totally honest before I met my twin flame, I had not heard of people such as Dr Wayne Dyer, Eckhart Tolle, Esther Hicks, or any other of the well known modern day spiritualists, and only through her introducing me to their work did I discover who they were. Until I put the page together, and then meeting my twin flame my spiritual world was a very narrow personal one, based around my own needs and experiences and served me well. What has happened since then still amazes me as nineteen months ago I could never have imagined what I would be doing today. It has been a total revelation and a massive awakening to me, and has given me a life purpose which I love.

I have also since watching and listening to many of the YouTube videos based around spirituality, had yet another rude awakening, in that as I watch them I am already fully aware of all the sayings and things they are teaching and talking about. It is already known to me, nothing they say is new. Maybe it is delivered in a different way and used in a different context, but I still find myself shocked at the knowing of what they all speak about.

Where have I gained all this knowing? Where has this spiritual knowledge come from? I can only presume I have gained this knowledge in a past life, and brought it with me for some purpose, but it gives me a strange feeling.

This is not my Ego screaming for acknowledgement as my ego only tends to appear when I get embarrassed because people give me compliments or praise for my work. I am very happy being who I am, being humble is my nature, and I find no reason to inflate my Ego as I'm no longer a young man trying to make his way in the human world or impress people and far too old to be bothered by Ego.

Neither am I somebody trying to raise their standing in the spiritual world as I am not interested in being some spiritual guru. I just love working with people.

I enjoy what I do, I connect with people through all that I say and write, and I just pass on my truths and the knowing from deep within me, my spirituality which people can take inspiration from or ignore, as it is their choice to do so.

I just look to help and support people through this difficult life journey and give them some spiritual understanding of that journey.

The reality of what has happened to bring me to this moment in my life has been a massive awakening in itself, but now fits like a comfortable pair of shoes and I am content in the knowledge that what I do really does touch people's lives and makes a difference to them, and I'm finally on my destined spiritual path, my reason for being here.

All that said, I have had a lifelong feeling that there was a purpose behind me being here and being pushed along towards it, and that this will be my last time here so that purpose will be achieved no matter what. It is just a knowing that all my guides and angels are working behind the scenes to ensure I reach this destined purpose.

At this moment or should I say in my now, my twin flame connection as difficult as it is, continues and flourishes even from 8000 miles apart, and the work I do with our many members grows in various ways. I firmly believe that whatever the purpose is for this incarnation my twin flame will play a major part in that journey, and why it was essential for us to meet. I just wish heaven could have organised it a little easier and sooner. Why have they had to wait so long and make it so difficult? I suppose that is divine timing for you and the purpose behind that timing we never know.

So now you know where I am at in this moment, and what is happening around all around me. This now leads me to the point of the book and telling you all the experiences and learning I have gone through that finally led to the existence of the page and my spiritual calling, a journey that has just begun in many ways.

If you believe the premise that before we arrive in this magnificent world that we have agreed and signed our soul contract for this incarnation and listed all the lessons we are here to learn, I can only reach the conclusion that I had a very long list and very in depth like I had a lot of cramming to do. As you will see from my life story it has been very full and intense at times, and I have learnt many lessons along the way, lessons I believe were essential to get me to reach the spiritual understanding I have finally arrived at, and the future path I am to tread. Hopefully as you tread my life path with me, you will not judge me for the decisions I have made, and hope you will gain something from it, even if your only awareness in the end, is that life is meant to flow and the best thing you can do, is let it.

"The Early Years"

I would imagine many of you would have heard of the story of Moses, found in a basket floating in the river. Likewise my start into this human life feels something like that, although I wasn't found floating in a river, but I did start life in a similar way with a situation of abandonment. The only information I know around my coming into this world and about my parents are the details which are written on my birth certificate, but how true they are, who knows? Although I experienced this abandonment by my parents I never once let it bother me, or get in the way of living my life. Acceptance and letting something go is a wonderful thing once you master it.

I was born on April 17th 1949, that bit I know to be true because as well as having my birth certificate I have also seen the official register along with my mother's signature, probably the closest I have ever felt to her.

I was born in the village branch of a major hospital in the county of Cheshire, England, to a married couple, according to the birth certificate. My father was a serving RAF corporal and my mother was of no known occupation, plus the birth certificate gave their address as being a local district within Greater Manchester.

I was 15 before I ever actually saw my birth certificate so I never even knew these details before then, and the only thing I knew throughout my young childhood was that I was fostered. From the age of around 5 when I started primary school, I was made aware of the reason why I had a different surname to my then foster parents even though I didn't really grasp or understand it. At least it wasn't kept a secret. They told me the story I was to know and grow up with until my twenties, which later I was to find out were all lies. The story I was told by my foster parents was that I was taken off my mother because she hit me repeatedly.

They said that because of her treatment towards me the local authorities stepped in and removed me from the family home, and I was then placed into my foster parents care at the age of 10 months old. That is it, the story I had to grow up with throughout my childhood and into my twenties and how I discovered anything more comes later in the story.

My foster parents were very working class and we were fairly poor even in comparison to other working class families, and although my foster father was a very hard working man. Times were always hard financially and my foster mother also worked part time as a cleaner at the local school. Somehow they managed to make ends meet, and the main thing I remember about my foster mother was her baking every Sunday, that filled the family home with this incredible smell, plus Sundays were usually the only day we ever saw anything that resembled a piece of meat.

We lived in a rented house on a privately owned housing estate, which if memory serves me right, my foster parents only got because my foster father used to be a night watchman while the estate was being built. A step up from a council estate and I remember that the house was far from being luxurious but was quite homely and comfortable. We didn't have the luxury of even a television until I was much older. My foster parents had 3 children of their own, all much older than me, but their two eldest children lived away from the family home, with their son being in the army overseas and I saw very little of him. Their eldest daughter was living with her soon to be husband in another city. The family home therefore, comprised of my foster parents, their youngest daughter and myself, and I was lucky enough to at least have my own bedroom which some other kids on the estate didn't have the luxury of.

I certainly cannot say my childhood was an unhappy one, because it really wasn't. Except for the odd outburst and falling out from my youngest foster sister, things were very normal at home in the main. I do remember once having a fight with my foster sister at the top of the stairs, and she fell down them. Fortunately she was only bruised, but I was grounded for a week.

I was brought up in a very caring neighbourhood, and in times when people were not afraid to leave their front doors open, so we lived in each other's houses as kids. Everybody was part of the community and knew each other's business, really cared and looked out for each other and everybody was your Aunt or Uncle.

The relationship I had with my foster parents is not what I would describe in any way as being an affectionately close one, as there was always the feeling of some distance between us that was not helped by my foster sister's comments. They were caring, and never once hit me, so at least I had a family to grow up in, unlike a lot of children that were taken into care at that time and lived in children's homes, I am very grateful for that.

My very early years are quite vague up to being around 5 year old just like most toddlers memories are. The only recollection I have of those early primary school years is a memory of some of the school teachers. I just loved the history teacher Mr Hughes a very lively jovial man, who triggered my first love of Greek Mythology through his teaching methods. He told us tales of Jason and the Argonauts, Jason and the Golden Fleece, and Helen of Troy, which somehow left a lasting impression. He was very much into Greek Mythology which I connected to and loved, even to this day. You can say it my very first connection to spirituality through these stories.

He encouraged us to act out the roles as he told the stories, which I loved doing, and little was I to know how much one of these stories would be linked to me some 60 plus years later. Through my tarot readings these early teachings come back to life as I use the Mythic Tarot deck, which is based around Greek mythology. In this deck the suit of Wands is linked to the story of Jason and the Golden Fleece and the previous knowledge of the story helped me in my learning of Tarot almost 40 years ago.

At around the age of eight, I started attending the church at bottom of our road on our estate and attended Sunday school like most of my local friends.

It was more a social thing than being a heavily religious experience as I was there with all my friends from the estate, plus the church also had a youth club, which only for those attending the church, so going was essential. At Sunday school, I actually got the reputation of being the disruptive one as I challenged every story told as a lot of the stories did not make sense to me. I also couldn't sit still for more than 2 minutes either because I was a very restless and adventurous child. Even at that age, I was to challenge most religious teachings, and I have been a challenger ever since of all things religious and spiritual. I am one of those people who has got to look at everything from every angle and fully understand it before accepting it.

In addition I was always at the centre of any mischief-making and I suppose a bit of a rebel and regularly got told off by the Sunday school teacher and several of my Primary school teachers even though I really loved school, a place where I didn't feel any different from any other child. My early years are still a bit of a distant memory except for an odd recollection now and then.

One of these recollections was from around the age of 8 or 9. I was playing with some friends on a canal bank, when suddenly I slipped and fell into the muddy canal. I was unable to swim at that age, and so just thrashed around trying to keep myself afloat.

The next thing I remember was this person pulling me back towards the bank and then out of the water to safety. The only thing I remember after this is being screamed at by my foster parents for being stupid, and I could have easily drowned had not this elderly man in his 60's seen what had happened and jumped in to save me. This, although not known at the time, was to be the first of 4 situations in which I should have died in my life, but it just wasn't my time.

At the age of eleven I moved up into the senior school and into the top stream class because I was quite intelligent, although failed my 11+ exam and so didn't get to go to grammar school like many of my friends. At church, I had become an Alter boy and started helping with every service, so life seemed to be moving along nicely without any problems and very normally. I was well-liked at both school and within the church community, but then life was to take a turn in a very unpleasant way and really because of my own doing. Whilst serving as an Alter boy, part of my duties was to take the collection plate after each service containing the money that had been donated by the congregation, from the Alter to the vestry.

In the vestry the vicar would count it and put it in the safe, which turned out to be a job I wished I had never been given. Coming from a poor family I had always envied most of my friends who always seemed to have everything I didn't have, and so I felt quite inferior at times and I suppose jealous.

This envy led me to go astray and after one of the Sunday services I started to steal from the collection plate to buy things with. I bought sweets and toys, just a little at first, but then more and more as I got away with it, and this went on for months taking some from each service.

One day and to my surprise the vicar who had obviously been suspecting something was going on, set a trap and marked a ten shilling note and placed it on the collection plate suspecting somebody was stealing, which I stupidly took. After the service when everybody had gone home I was confronted by him and he asked me straight out if I had been stealing from the collection. Being absolutely petrified I first denied it, but he asked me to empty my pockets, and so the note was found.

I remember being filled with remorse and guilt at being caught doing this and then bursting into tears fearful of the consequences. The vicar was fuming at me for stealing but said he would let it go this time and he would work out a suitable punishment but I had to promise that I would never do it again.

I was so relieved that nobody was to find out and I wouldn't be disgraced, but unfortunately that was not to be the end of it, and it would be used against me to keep me silent as events unfolded. Somewhere around a month or so after this event and when I thought the event was firmly in the past, I found myself in the vestry all alone with the vicar after a service when everybody else had left the building.

I can still recall it as though it was yesterday, and an experience I could never forget.

The vicar moved towards me with a peculiar look on his face and thought he was just going to tell me off for something. Instead he put his hand on my shoulder and pinned me up against a wall and he started to sexually abuse me.

I remember being frozen to the spot, not really understanding what was happening, but I can even remember the smell of the strong French cigarettes he smoked as he breathed on me as he pushed himself against me, it was a strong disgusting smell.

This was to be my first sexual encounter of any kind and I really wasn't sure about how I should feel because I was so innocent and nobody had ever spoken about sex let alone abuse in those days, and I just had no knowledge about any of it. It lasted for about 10minutes and after it was all over I was in some kind of shock at what he had done, but he told me to keep it a secret. Nobody needed to know it would be our secret, just as he would keep my stealing a secret so parents wouldn't find out or the police arrest me.

This went on just about every week for several months and at every opportunity, he would even get me passes from school to serve at weekday funerals. Although I felt unsure and uneasy at what he was doing, I was helpless to do anything about it or tell anybody. I actually didn't even know if this was normal adult behaviour or not, I was just too young to understand and very confused. I did all I could to avoid being alone with him, but it wasn't easy as I was still carrying the guilt of being caught stealing in my head. After around 3 or 4 months it just stopped and I will never know if he just got scared of being caught, or he had moved on to another unsuspecting Alter boy, but at least my ordeal was over and it had ceased for me and life could get back to normal. I sort of put the whole experience at the back of my mind and moved on normally.

At around the age of twelve, it was discovered that I had not been baptised as a baby, which in those times was normal in working class families, and as I had been in care it and been totally overlooked.

As my foster parents were in no way religious they hadn't even given it any thought. However, at church you couldn't receive Holy Communion unless you had been baptised, so baptism was essential.

The baptism date was arranged, and 3 males had to be appointed from within the church community to become my godfathers. I was allowed to choose one and so I chose my best friend from the road where I lived who also went to the church, another was just a random member of the church community whom knew me and volunteered after a request was put out, and the third was the church's curate who was chosen by the vicar. The date was arranged and the baptism took place and my foster parents had absolutely nothing to do with it even though they were invited by the vicar.

A few weeks after the baptism, one of my Godfathers who also worked for a local shop delivering groceries during the day invited me to go for a day out with him in the van to the countryside. He knew that I had never been in a car before because I had mentioned it when talking to him previously. So this was an offer I jumped at because besides never having been in a car before I also had never been into the real countryside before because we lived in the inner city. I really thought that he was just being nice as my newly appointed Godfather, but this was also to be an adventure I would never forget. We drove into the countryside and he had even brought some food along for lunch and he found a nice quiet spot overlooking farmland to sit and eat the food, where there was nobody else around but us.

I really don't want to go into detail about this or sensationalise it in any way, the only thing I will say is that he also abused me.

Again after he had finished with me I was told in no uncertain terms not to tell anybody about what had happened because they would never believe me as he was a curate, a man of the church and I would be shamed for lying.

I was just so trusting and so naive unlike a 12 year old would be today, and yet again somebody had abused and blackmailed me into silence. Something I acknowledge now in retrospect is that I am happy that child abuse is now an openly discussed situation so that children are aware and don't have to feel ashamed or feel scared about reporting it. Fortunately this only happened once with my Godfather and I didn't have to face him at the Sunday services for very long, as he soon moved out of the district and away from the church.

This made it easier for me to shut it out of my everyday existence, and even though I do not know how I did it, I was able to put it all behind me and move on with my young life. I still think even at that young age I blamed myself for bringing it all about through stealing in the first place, but burying these experiences at the back of my mind as if they had never happened was the only solution.

By the age of around thirteen, I became good friends with four girls who lived up the road with their widowed mother Irene who we all called Ma. My connection to the girls and in turn to their mother was to provide my first encounter with the spiritual world as I became sort of part of the family and spent lots of time at their house. Their mother was a small but bubbly person who always had a smile on her face and a meal on the table for anybody that needed it, no matter how hard things were.

I was soon to discover that she read playing cards for people which was regarded as fortune telling in those days, the original way of reading cards derived from the Romany Gypsy's which has virtually now died out.

As I was an inquisitive child and always asking questions, she took the time to explain to me the basics of each suit which run parallel to today's Tarot suits, and also gave me a brief understanding of how to do a reading although I didn't quite grasp it or what intuition was. In addition, she explained briefly the basics of her belief in spiritualism and what it meant to her, and that she went every week to a spiritualist church to be amongst likeminded people of similar beliefs.

In my young mind her beliefs made more sense to me than all the religious stuff I had been taught at church which I could never get my head round, and I accepted it. There were many occasions when she would send us out of the room because she said that spirit wanted to talk to her, and although it seemed a little spooky at first it eventually became normal to just accept it, and I never felt uncomfortable about it.

This was to be my introduction to the world of spirituality and the start of my interest around spiritualism which stayed with me in the back of my mind.

In retrospect this was like the sowing of the spiritual seed which would stay in the dark until it was time to germinate. My tender early years had really opened my eyes to the world, firstly to the way people could act and behave towards one another, abuse them and make them feel helpless and confused, this being the bad side. On the good side, I had my awakening to spiritualism and the spirit world which was to stay permanently in my life and almost 60 years later give me so much purpose. By the age of 15 my foster father had to give up work because of ill health. My foster mother suffered with severe arthritis and had to also give up her job as a cleaner. My youngest foster sister also got married and moved out of the family home and therefore the house was now too big for three people and so we moved to a smaller flat on the same estate.

Financial problems grew at home and even though I was really bright and doing well at school my foster mother told me I would have to leave school and get a job to help support the family, laying the guilt trip on me that they had looked after me for 15 years and now it was my turn to look after them. To say I was unhappy about this would be an understatement as I was very upset and aggrieved as I really loved going to school, and especially doing technical drawing because I always wanted to become a draughtsman or architect.

In the end, after pleading my corner I gave up the fight and I left school at 15 to get a job. I managed to get a job fairly quickly at the new Tesco supermarket that had just opened nearby as a shelf stacker. Not my dream job, but at least it was a job and I was grateful to get it as I had no qualifications.

My train of thought was as supermarkets were a new thing of the era away from the usual small local corner shops we were used to, being a big store employing around 60 staff I thought it would offer some chance of gaining a promotion if I worked hard.

By the time I was fifteen and a half and although I had already gained a promotion to supervisor in those first 6 months I was extremely unhappy at work and didn't really like it. I was also increasingly unhappy at home feeling like I was only there being used as a money making machine.

I was looking for a way to move my life forward in some way. One day, I bumped into an ex school friend who was a little older than me and who had joined the army. He was home on leave and feeling very proud stood there in his uniform having just finished his training. He told me how in 2 weeks he would be joining his regiment in Germany, and I thought how good that would be, so I had that light bulb moment.

This was how I could change my life and get away. It was like somebody opening a door and showing me freedom, a freedom I so desired.

After a couple of days toying with the idea and plucking up the courage, I went down to the local army recruitment office on my day off work to get all the details about joining. I had to arrange to go back again a few days later to take the entry exam, again because I had no qualifications from school but which in the end I happily passed with flying colours. After the exam I learnt that I could join as what they called a boy soldier because I was not yet 16, but when I reached 16 I could then go on and join a regiment of my choice. As I had done so well in the entrance exam they advised me to go into the cavalry which they considered were the elite of the army and which were actually the tank regiments of that time.

They also told me that training would be at least 20 weeks so by the time I was trained I would have reached the age of 16, so there would be no wait getting into a regiment. As I sat talking to the recruiting sergeant major who was very keen on me joining we stumbled on the only problem, that my foster parents would have to agree to me joining because I was under 16, they were my legal guardians. I explained how they had made me leave school and their need for my income and so I thought they might not agree to me joining.

The sergeant major said he would come home with me and try and persuade them, which he did, and after long discussions and me agreeing to have half my pay deducted and sent home every month, he finally convinced them of the advantages and they signed the papers. After all they would be getting regular payments and not even have to feed or house me, win-win for them.

Feeling very happy, two weeks later, I was boarding a train heading for the army training camp in the far north of England with a feeling of freedom and growth, and looking forward to becoming a soldier, and a new life that was now before me.

I was also putting behind me all the traumas of my early years and thinking at that point that all these experiences were maybe just normal growing up and probably everybody went through the same. Why would I be any different?

In Retrospect

The early years of a child are supposed to be the happiest moments of its life, and even as I look back at my childhood and everything that happened to me, I cannot say that I didn't have a reasonably happy childhood. I was clothed, fed, had friends, and grew up in a very caring neighbourhood with some lovely people around me.

The fact I didn't have maternal parents never really bothered me in my early years as I still had a home and a family of sorts, so didn't feel neglected.

Yes, we were poor, and I missed out on the material things all my friends seemed to have but there can be no excuse for stealing. I still recognise all the things that happened to me as a youngster were the result of my own actions brought on through greed and envy, and as such were a very good early lesson to learn in life.

The abuse I suffered from the two men, was an abuse of power over a child and is inexcusable. I was asked today by my twin flame what did I actually felt emotionally about what happened, and I will say here exactly what I said to her, "I felt nothing", I just didn't understand what was happening me. You have to understand that we didn't have sex education in those days and child sexual abuse was never spoken or heard of, so there was no awareness, no understanding.

Strangely enough it was probably a good thing in a roundabout stupid sort of way, as I never stole another thing in my life, and I can't remember ever being envious of anybody again throughout my life, which shows that some lessons can be learnt from the most difficult situations. This realisation enabled me to pass through the experience without long lasting mental scars, just confusion around sex and sexual identity. It also goes to show that sometimes in Life ignorance can be bliss, and to dissect everything that happens into its smallest components only causes you to magnify it out of proportion and keep you attached to it. In my case I was also able to learn about detachment and just let it go, even though for many years I still blamed myself for what happened.

With regards to my foster parents I didn't know at the time that they were paid by social services to look after me like many foster parents are even today. Therefore to them I was just a job, another income source but still providing a service and giving a temporary home to children in need, and they did a very good job of it.

There is nowhere in a fostering agreement that says it is compulsory to love a foster child, although it would be normally accepted that this is the reason why you foster in the first place, but neither does it say that at 15 the child has to look after you in return. My foster parents were selfish in their actions to make me leave school and start work at 15, particularly as I was doing well at school, and could have gone on to get qualified and had a much better career, and also stayed at home longer, but it is was what it was, because nothing can ever change it. There is actually no point looking back at the things that happened in the past because no matter how much there is regret nothing can change it, so detach, let go and just keep moving your life forward.

What did I learn spiritually from the experiences I went through in this phase of my life? Well, because of my age I don't think anything came to mind at that time. I was just too young. However, in retrospect, I can find a couple things.

Firstly, from leaving my home and my foster parents. This is about acknowledging that when something or someone no longer serves you or brings you joy, you should just put it behind you and move on with your life. Do not be fearful about change because if you just accept the flow of life there can be many amazing things around the next corner. It is said that when a situation no longer brings you joy, change it, if you can't change it, leave it, and this is a lesson that I took through my life without even realising it.

Secondly, when we are born we only know how to love and laugh. We have no cares, and a child doesn't know of the existence of fear energy and therefore is open to the natural flow of life and just takes everything in its stride and lives in the now.

Only when adults start to impress their views, attitudes, and actions upon a child does the child start to lose this natural flow for life and start being fearful of the future. Change is a natural process in life if we are not to stagnate, we were not born to stay in one place, and you will learn nothing from being in one place.

One thing I did learn up to this point is that we are here to learn lessons, some will good but some will be bad. The Universe has planned it in such a way, that if we don't learn the lesson the first time it will keep recurring until you do learn it.

Had I had the courage to report the vicar in the first place, and been prepared to accept the consequences of my actions in stealing, then the second occurrence would never have happened, so I learnt this lesson the hard way.

Remember the biggest block to change is fear energy, all the what if's, and maybe's, if we were to consider changing anything.

Fear energy is just an illusion because the future has not arrived and you can't predict what is in wait for you to meet so don't fear change, just let life flow in its natural way and enjoy and make the most of the journey. If something does go wrong, pick yourself up, dust yourself off, let it go and start again.

"The Young Man"

My train ride to the army training camp felt like a ride to freedom, a journey into manhood with a big new world to discover. After a few hours travelling I arrived at the Garrison training camp full of excitement for this new found freedom and this new adventure. I had not a clue what I was going to face or go through during the training or what life had in store for me afterwards. This was just another big stepping stone forward on my journey of life.

The intake of new soldiers I was to join consisted of males from my age up to 25 years old all in the same boat, all leaving their normal home life behind them and on a new journey in life. Filled with both excitement and fear of the unknown and what was in store, these guys were from all walks of life and backgrounds, and we now all had the same thing in common, we were all new to the army and going to be living the same life no matter what our background. The only thing we were told on day one was that it would be tough, it would long days, and that some would not make it. Every 4 weeks we would undertake a physical endurance test which we had to pass in order to complete our training. We were then marched off to get our hair cut and to be kitted out with our army clothing and uniforms. I very quickly made friends with the guys around my own age and got stuck into the training, learning very quickly to keep my head down and not stand out to much. Those who tried to be tough guys in front of everybody, and the "know it all's" suffered badly at the hands of the troop sergeant, quite often being shamed in front of the whole platoon, and brought down to size. I saw many big strong guys with attitude being broken down and brought to tears on the parade ground as the drill sergeant humiliated them.

We lost a few of the weaker guys each and every month, with them being made to leave the army altogether as they failed their physical tests. So I just did as I was told, took everything on board that I was taught or told to do, and got on with being the best I could be at everything given me.

After being there for around 2 months we were told that we were to be visited by Queen Elizabeth the Queen's mother, so the whole camp had to be spruced up. It was at this point I got myself into the first lot of trouble in my army career.

On a night whilst out in the local garrison town of Richmond with a bunch of my army friends, I got a little drunk for the first time in my life, and full of drunken bravado I hoisted a pair of union Jack underpants up the flagpole of the old castle in the town centre.

The castle was the towns centre piece and pride and joy, as well as being a big tourist attraction for the town.

Big mistake!! Local residents complained in droves to the camp and so I had to own up to my actions so that punishment wouldn't be doled out to everybody. My punishment was harsh, and I was to whitewash hundreds of stone boulders that were used as edging stones around the camp using only a toothbrush and they gave me a week to complete the task, which meant working from early morning until late into each night until I finally finished it.

The day of the Queen Mothers visit came with a great buzz around the place, and we were lined up on the parade ground to welcome her and for her inspection.

As she walked through the ranks I saw her approaching through the corner of my eye and to my absolute shock she stopped in front of me and started to talk to me.

I remember her being very gently spoken and seemed very interested in where I was from and why I had joined the army, and the conversation seemed to go on for ages although it was only actually a few minutes. I remember a sense of pride at being the one chosen to talk to her, but little did she know about what I'd done the week before! She may have even seen the funny side, who knows?

After what seemed like an eternity the 20 weeks of hard training came to an end and we arrived at the day of the passing out parade where we would be recognised as fully trained soldiers. At the passing out parade family and friends were invited to come and celebrate with their young men. I was the only soldier whose parents or relatives were not there to congratulate them, which really took the shine off my pride of going through all the training and it really hit home that feeling of not being wanted or belonging. This was probably the only time in my life I have had a recognition of not having my own real parents, when I really wanted and needed them there.

As I had now reached the age of 16, I was allocated to the same tank regiment that my school friend had joined and was based in West Germany. Before I was to join them

I was given 2 weeks leave, and so full of pride I headed home to Manchester not knowing what to expect as I was returning home a man, young, but still now a man in my own right.

As I arrived home at my foster parent's home I vividly remember the very first statement that came out of my foster mother's mouth, "when are you going back? Not how are you? Or what was training like? I remember a real feeling of being unwanted and unloved, like I just wasn't wanted there.

As I had spent very little of my earnings during training I was able to give her some extra money to cover my food cost while I was home, which seemed to put her at ease and change her mood.

Because of the ill feelings at home I spent most of my leave with the 4 girls Christine, Sally, Jean, and Irene that I had grown up with on the estate and their lovely spiritual mother, Irene. Without me telling her, Irene just knew that there was a problem at home, and accepted me like a long lost son, and like part of her family without any hesitation. At this point little was I to know how this coming together as part of her family would impact on her daughter's lives in the years to come.

Back in my foster parents home the feeling of being unwanted continued with a very uneasy atmosphere and very few words spoken between us, so when the day came to fly out back to Germany and to my regiment I was relieved to be leaving my foster parents. I was also sad to be leaving my newly adopted family behind who had made me feel so welcome and so part of their family.

I took my first flight ever in an old Dakota aeroplane which was like a rattling tin can with wings which was often referred to as the sit up and beg plane, and the 2 hour flight was very scary, being my first experience of flying. I eventually arrived after around 5 hours travelling at my regimental camp based in Paderborn West Germany. Presenting myself to the guardhouse I was allocated and shown to "C" company, and put into a 6 man room with 5 other experienced soldiers, and I remember feeling that this was the start of my new life. Here I was in the army, a very man's world, in a different country, with so much to discover, and my new room friends soon brought me up to speed with daily routines.

I settled very quickly into the daily routine, and our working day came as somewhat of a shock especially after the gruelling training days, as we only worked from 8am until 4.30 Monday to Friday, with a half day on Wednesdays for sports and not at all at weekends unless you had the misfortune of being on guard duty.

Not at all what I expected after how training had been it was just like a normal job, and there was enormous opportunity and free time to go and discover both the town and everything the country had to offer.

After being there around 6 months I got a little drunk and started reflecting on home, and so one night I sat down and wrote to my foster parents. I thanked them for raising me but explained that I no longer wanted anything to do with them, as they had made me feel so unwelcomed and unwanted when I was on leave. I also went on to inform them that I was stopping the money going home to them as I considered it unfair on me and that there was never any thanks for me doing so. I know that this action sounds mean or cruel, and you need to understand that they were paid for looking after me as a child by the local authorities, it was not done out of love, and they did have 3 children of their own to help look after them if they needed help. In the end they did a job of work and were paid for doing so, and now their job had come to an end and I needed to find my own identity and rightful independence.

It was at my next leave that I was to encounter and discover the reality of somebody being a spiritual medium. I went back home on leave with the thought that my new found family would let me stay at their house and sleep on the settee for a few days. I was to get an immediate shock as I knocked on the door. It was opened by my newly adopted mother Irene.

As she opened the door she outstretched her hand which had a key on it, followed by the words "I think you will be needing that". In a state of surprise I immediately asked "how do you know?" and the reply came "I know more than you could imagine" and that is all she said about it. All of a sudden and totally out of nowhere, It was like I had found a new home, a new family, and this home was filled with so much love and care, something I had experienced very little of in my life. This I feel was the first real example of my guides showing me their presence in my life and being there when I needed them the most.

I had a great leave filled with lots of laughter, and it all felt very comfortable now being an adopted member of this family.

When the leave came to an end, all of the girls gave me photos to take back with me to stick on my locker, to remind me that I had a family and a home to always come back to, and it was all quite moving, but again, little was I to know at that point what would happen because of this.

Wanting to cut a long story short, all my newly adopted sisters were very attractive blonde haired blue eyed girls and many of the lads who saw the pictures on my locker, instantly fell in love, and asked about them, and if it was possible that they could write to them, which I arranged with the girls' permission.

Over the next 2 years each girl developed a relationship with one of my army colleagues and all ended up marrying them. Rather than repeating this story later on, I will tell you the outcome of these relationships now. Unfortunately it is not easy being married to somebody in the army because of separation time, and all the girls eventually ended up divorcing.

One of the couples managed to have a child in that time, a little girl called Samantha and she grew up to be a very lovely young woman the last time I saw her. So my life had been filled with many ups and downs to this point, and I had now been in the army for just under 3 years. I was now a young man of 19, with hormones raging as they do, but still very confused, as I had no knowledge of a sexual life.

The only thing I had experienced was the same sex sexual encounters of my younger life which had been forced upon me, and I had never had a girlfriend or any close relationship. In this very confused state of mind I made a move on a young man about the same age, as me who instantly rebuffed me and left the room calling me all sorts of names. He went and told a couple of the other men and before long it spread around most of the company and from then on my life became a living nightmare. I was verbally and physically bullied, my bed was regularly tipped upside down while I was sleeping in it, which was horrifying and

I became increasingly scared for my safety as the bullying continued.

I couldn't complain or tell anybody in authority what was happening because everything would have to come out into the open and being "queer" as they called it in those days was a court marshal offence, not that I was, I was just in a very confused place. It got to the point where I couldn't take it anymore and I snapped, the result being I packed a bag and ran away, as it was the only solution I could come up with. After a couple days travelling I made it back to England by trains and ferry and ended up in the centre of London a very big and lonely city.

I had very little money left and even less idea what I was going to do, but at least I was away from all the bullying.

I couldn't go back to my home town of Manchester because that would be the first place that the military police would be looking for me.

Here I was in the capital city, all alone with almost no money, and no idea of what I was going to do from here on in. After a few of days of walking the streets of London day and night I completely ran out of money and started to get very hungry, I was unwashed and dirty and feeling very lonely.

One night, I was sitting on a bench in Charing Cross train station, because at night it was a warmer and safer place to be. As I sat there feeling very sorry for myself and very hungry, a young guy around the age of 30 came and sat next to me.

He introduced himself as Mark and he started chatting asking me where I was from and what I was doing in London. I must have looked terrible because I felt it, and I remember telling him some cock and bull story that I was in London looking for work but had run out of money and not eaten for a day or so.

He said if I wanted to I could go back to his place and have a shower, and that he would make some food for me, an offer I jumped at as I was desperate. I even had a knowing that he was gay even though there were no outwardly visible signs. I just knew at the back of my mind what he wanted in return, it really did not take much intuition to work that out, and yes I spent the night in his bed.

I had gone beyond the point of caring, it was just survival, I just needed food, needed a shower, and to get off the streets for a night and have a proper sleep, anything else did not matter. Pride, self respect, and everything else went out the window as the survival instinct kicked in.

The following morning I woke up at around 9 am having had the best night's sleep I'd had in ages. Mark had got up without me even noticing and gone to work, leaving me a note which said, "help yourself to breakfast, thank you for last night, I have left you some luncheon vouchers on the table so you can get food for the next couple of days, good luck with your search for work, and please make sure the door to the flat is closed firmly when you leave". In a way I was very grateful for what he'd done for me, at least I was a little revived and felt better.

So there I was, back on the streets of this enormous City wondering what I was going to do, or where I would go. Later that day the most extraordinary thing happened.

I returned to Charing Cross Station in the early evening, and even sat on the same bench, and like before a guy came and sat next to me. This time he was a much older man, very respectable looking, well dressed, and well spoken, and carrying a briefcase looking very business-like. We got chatting, and I spun him the same line I had told Mark, and after around thirty minutes chatting he turned and said, "I don't know if you would be interested, but I have a job for you, and you can come and stay with me and my family until we find you a place to live".

I could have hugged him, it was like an angel from heaven had just landed in front of me, an angel called Ron. He went and bought me a train ticket to his village in the heart Kent and off we went on this new unknown adventure.

It was about a 30 minute train ride, and we eventually arrived at his home just outside this beautiful little village called Paddock Wood in Kent.

I was feeling a little nervous and apprehensive, but also thinking "what have I got to lose? Anything has to be better than the streets of London."

He introduced me to his family and repeated the story I had told him to his wife and two sons who were both much younger than me, and we all sat down to a meal at the table. I was so hungry, and I remember feeling very strange and it all felt very surreal, like I was dreaming, but after dinner we sat down and he explained the job he had for me which sounded really interesting.

He worked freelance for an American insurance company interviewing Americans in the UK who had applied for insurance from the company he was working for.

He had far more work coming in than he could handle as these people he needed to interview were all over the South of England, so it involved a lot of travelling and he couldn't handle it all. He spent a couple of days training me up, showing me all the paperwork and how to complete them. He then set me to work travelling all over the southern counties, meeting some very interesting people along the way including pop stars, American soldiers based in England, and people from all walks of life.

After a few weeks and me doing a good job, he bought a second hand caravan which he positioned on land at the back of his house for me to live in which would give me some privacy and which was so much nicer than sleeping on the settee. We worked together for around four or five months until one day he told me that the work was drying up and that I would have to find another job although I could still live in the caravan. I was very sad as I enjoyed the work. Not being one who is afraid of change I got off my butt and went job hunting, and very quickly found a job within a few days in the village supermarket and so I started working there the very next week.

After working for Ron, and having a lot of freedom, the work at the supermarket was very boring, very mundane, but a job was a job.

After only a couple of weeks working there I became very attracted to a young lady called Janet who worked on the checkout at the supermarket and who was very friendly towards me. She was around the same age as me. She was pretty, shorter than myself, had a very soft voice, and a smile that just melted you.

It wasn't very long before I plucked up courage to ask her out and fortunately she said yes and we started going out together. She lived at home with her parents and brother within the village, not far from work and her brother used to drive me home each time I went out with Janet, as I lived on the outskirts of the village and didn't have transport to get myself home, and so getting any alone time together was virtually impossible.

Most of our dates were spent in the village pub with her brother and his girlfriend, as there really wasn't much else going on nearby so I decided to go hunting for a flat to give us some privacy. I eventually found one in the nearby town, which was only one stop on the train to work each day. Janet was able to get to my place the same way and it was only 5 minutes on the train. Although things improved and we managed to get some alone time it never went too far sexually, I'm still not sure why because I was very attracted to her and we did get into heavy petting on occasions, but never went the whole way.

The one thing she did make me realise was that I was definitely heterosexual even though the right moment to advance our relationship to a more physical one never arose. Life seemed to be moving along very nicely, and I had been living in the flat for about two months totally enjoying life, then one morning at around 6am there was a loud knock at the door.

Shocked and half asleep I opened the door only to find that two police officers were stood there, who announced that they had come to take me in because they had been informed that I was absent without leave from the army, and they had been instructed to return me. They gave a few minutes to gather my clothes together into a back pack, and off we went to the police station, where I was held for around 8 hours before the military police came to collect me. They in turn took me to a military camp where I was held for 3 days before being escorted back to my regiment in Germany.

I had been absent in total for around 7 months and had discovered a lot about myself - especially that I wasn't gay, but just a normal heterosexual guy, which I suppose was what I was looking to resolve and find out one way or another.

Apparently, the army had located me through the taxation system, something I hadn't given any thought to when I took the job at the supermarket, but it's only by making mistakes we ever learn. Needless to say this was also the end of my relationship with Janet because I had never told her the truth of how I came to be in the South of England, and although I wrote to her, she never replied.

After I was returned to my regiment in Germany, they deposited me into the regimental guard room, and from there, I was put in front of my commanding officer who allowed me to remain soldiering awaiting a Court Marshal. It took 4 weeks for the Court Marshal to be scheduled, and all the regimental police started taking bets on how long they thought my sentence in military prison would be. I believe the minimum that was bet on was 6 months in Colchester military Prison, so I soldiered on within my company awaiting my fate.

The adjutant, a Captain, was appointed to defend me at my court marshal and he was a really nice man and very understanding so I told him my story, the truth, the whole truth, and nothing but the truth, explaining everything that had happened leading up to making me go absent. He was very sympathetic to my reason for running away and said we had a very solid plea for mitigation.

The day came all too soon and we arrived at the place the court marshal was to be held. On the day and all through

49

the case my defence officer was absolutely incredible, and I couldn't have wished for a better person to defend me, he even had me in tears as he told my story with compassion and understanding. He made the whole thing sound like the army had let me down because they had allowed such bullying to go on, and after they adjourned to weigh the case up. It took just 20 minutes for the panel of senior officers presiding over the Court Marshal to deliver a verdict, and I sat there petrified of what sentence I would be given. The thought of military prison scared me to death as the prisons reputation was well known as being a hell hole for its prisoners. I was asked to stand, and a verdict of guilty for being absent without leave was pronounced followed by a statement that because of the extenuating circumstances, a sentence of only 28 days was to be awarded to be served in my regimental jail. I even received a sort of apology for how the army had let me down in not being there to support me when I needed it the most. What relief, I nearly collapsed on the spot in shock and I remember thinking to myself "who says there isn't a God?" because he surely had a part to play in what had just happened! Heaven had sent me yet another Angel to protect me in the guise of my defending officer, who I thanked profoundly. I also thanked Heaven.

I remember going back to the regimental jail full of relief that it was now all over and with a smile back on my face. I took great pleasure announcing my sentence to the regimental police and that none of them had won the bet. I will never forget their looks of disbelief and disappointment on their faces as I announced my 28 day sentence, although I also thought they might make my 28 day sentence very hard as their way of getting revenge.

The very next day after breakfast, I was told to report to the regimental sergeant major's office for duties, unaware that the adjutant had been and had a word with him and asked him to make things easy for me to serve my sentence and I was to be allocated to work for him every day during my sentence instead of being drilled, doing kitchen duties, or litter picking duties which most prisoners had to do.

Instead, I would look after his uniform, tidy his office, run errands, and occasionally drive his wife supermarket shopping. In fact, life was made very easy for me and I only spent the nights in the jail to sleep, so how could I not realise that my angels and guides were always around me, taking care of me? How could I not feel their presence through everything I had gone through?

I remember looking back at my life up to this point, trying to make sense of it all, but one thing I became fully aware of, was that something was at work in my life, looking after me, guiding me, and protecting me.

Yes, I still had my lessons to learn, but they certainly made it easier for me, and I got this immense feeling that it would all be for a purpose at some point. It felt like I was being guided. This real feeling of being guided for a purpose, which at some point would all be made clear to me.

I could now see how something was always there moving me away from situations that could have turned out to be very nasty or putting the right people in the right place at the right time. An absolutely massive spiritual awakening, and genuine acknowledgement of the existence of spirit in my life.

Something else I came to an understanding about, was that I didn't join the army to play at being Soldiers, in fact

I was anti violence of any sort, let alone being able to shoot somebody, and I had only joined the army to get away from my foster family and discover life and myself.

When my sentence was served, I rejoined my company and decided to start living for me and going out there and discovering all the joy I could cram into my life.

On the first morning on parade after rejoining my company, the company sergeant major gave a very stern lecture to everybody about what would happen to anybody found bullying, which made me realise that what had been said at the Court marshal had been filtered down through the regiment, and to my surprise the incident was never brought up again and normal life resumed.

With the promise to myself in mind I used all my free time and the last 2 years of my service, to fill it with as much Joy and fun as I could possibly find.

I learnt to play guitar, formed a band called "The Strange" and we played all over Germany, in pubs, clubs, even various different sergeant's mess's of other regiments. In fact we would play anywhere and at every opportunity. We even came home to the UK and played 28 nights on a row in various youth centres on behalf of the army, to show that even being in the forces you can also have a fun life.

We had the advantage that the adjutant who defended me at my court marshal also became the group's manager, so getting time off for these things became easy.

Besides that I worked in a young person's bar in the city where we were based, and also did some work as a DJ at various local discos, in fact anything but play soldiers. I even paid other guys to cover my guard duties when I was listed to do them, no way was I playing "soldiers."

During this fun time I also developed a relationship with a beautiful young German girl called Annalese, who lived in the town sharing an apartment with her sister.

Her father was one of the wealthiest men in Germany owning the nation's largest bakery, but it all became very serious very quickly and she started talking about marrying, which made me run for the hills as I was petrified of that sort of commitment being so young and having only just really found myself. Marriage and commitment was the last thing on my mind. I just wanted to have fun after everything that I had gone through before, and I just didn't want that kind of responsibility and so eventually we parted, so she could go and find somebody who wanted the same thing as her.

The regiment was posted back to Andover in the UK for the last 6 months of my service and every weekend I used to go to the roundhouse in London with my drummer friend Graham from the band, to watch live groups all day on the Sunday. The band had broken up and this was a way to continue with my love of music.

I went on to keep my promise to myself and to fill the last 2 years of my 6 year service grabbing all the fun and joy I could have, and living in the now.

All too soon the fun was over and those 2 years passed and it was time to go back to the real world and civilian life. I could have signed on for another 3 years if I had wanted, but I thought the time had come to go and discover civilian and real life again, but this time as an adult and ready to take on the world.

In Retrospect

So much happened in this period of my life and I discovered that life and situations can change in the blink of an eye and nothing is written in stone or predictable.

Life is meant to flow and we should just let it, nothing can be assumed or predicted, especially the outcomes of change, and therefore getting yourself into a spiral of fear energy because of changes either chosen or enforced serves no purpose.

All the fears you build up around change are just fantasies, they are just an illusion you create and will not reflect the reality when it occurs.

The reality compared to the fear you build up and what is actually lying in wait around the corner may just surprise you as I have seen up to this point.

If you are confronted with a difficult situation it is a lesson for you to learn from. It is not a life sentence and you will pass through it. Learn the lesson so that you don't have to repeat it, acknowledge your part in the lesson that you have been shown, and if need be forgive yourself for your part and other people involved for theirs and never form an attachment to what has gone before. See it for what it was, and let it go. We are human and will make mistakes, and you're allowed to make mistakes. Nobody is perfect, don't beat yourself up when you make one just acknowledge that it was an essential part of learning the lesson you have been confronted with.

On a spiritual level this period contained several lessons or awakenings as I prefer to call them, as I believe that through experiencing many things in life and learning many lessons we can be drawn inexplicably onto our spiritual paths, Your awakening doesn't have to be one single light bulb moment, your awakening can be like mine, spread out over a much greater period of time, with little incidents and experiences making you more aware of something working in your life and drawing you closer to your consciousness.

I also learnt that giving and compassion are an essential quality and part of living a spiritual life within a world so selfish and messed up, something I have been shown during this period, plus that upon this earth walk many Earth angels who just give because of their unconditional love for humanity.

This was a major period when I really started to feel that someone or something was at work in my life, helping me and guiding me through some very difficult times, and ensuring that I always had enough, or as one door shut another would open.

I began to feel that everything happening to me was for a reason, and that so much more was waiting to be discovered, and I would never fear change again. You might even say that law of attraction had started to show its face at this point, not that things just fell out of the sky, but I understood and knew what I was wanting in my life, and what I was not wanting. I was prepared to work hard towards everything I wanted, and so my vibration attracted those things that were in alignment with it, and my life improved. Since this period I also look to balance my Karma, by giving help to those who need help, repaying the help I was given, and thus changing people's lives just like mine was changed by those who supported me when I needed it.

All these life experiences brought me to the understanding that if you want the best out of life then you should live by the rule of "Always treat people in exactly the same way that you would expect to be treated" and if you follow this rule you will not go far wrong.

Also I want you to remember that you are here to live your life in alignment with what feels right for you, and you are not responsible for the thoughts or actions of others, only how you react to them. Your life is your life, theirs is their life, and you live your life for you, it is your experience to have.

No human is perfect enough to judge another. Just be the best you can be at being a human and give your spirit the best human experience it can have.

In the words of Lao Tzu, "New beginnings are often disguised as painful endings."

"A Return to Normal Life"

The day arrived when I had to say goodbye to the army. And I headed home back to Manchester and it was only on the train ride home that the realisation hit me - that I really had nowhere to go, no real home, no real family, Manchester was the only place I knew and felt I belonged. It felt like shedding a familiar life for a new unknown future and with everything that happened up to this moment there was some trepidation at what may lay ahead.

During the last 2 years of being in the army, I learnt via a third party that both my foster parents had died, and that all the girls from my other family were now living back at home after their divorces so there may not be room for me anymore and would that impact on how they thought about me, I realised I had to come up with a plan pretty quick.

I remember arriving in Manchester city centre standing in a taxi rank with the temperature somewhere in the minus degrees, shivering, and feeling somewhat alone and it was very daunting. I had decided to brave it, and go to my new adopted families home and ask for the settee to sleep on for a couple of nights in order to give me a chance of finding somewhere to live, which on arrival at their house and to my relief, I was still welcomed with open arms. After all the upset with the divorces, I wasn't sure if things would have been fine. Fortunately I had enough money to obtain and rent a small bed sit apartment in the not so prestigious part of the city, at least I had a roof over my head and a bed to sleep in which I could call mine. Next was to find a job and I scoured the papers for days until I stumbled on a job in a factory that manufactured tanks for the army, and because I had served 6 years in a tank regiment, landing the job was easy.

Within a very short time I now had a place to call home, a job to pay for it, and things were looking up already. The only thing that was missing now was some companionship and friendship to fill the empty hours when I wasn't working, so I decided to go visit some of my old school day friends I had grown up with on my estate. Before long, I had established contact with a few good friends from my childhood and we met virtually every evening at the local pub in the area I had grown up in.

As we talked, it seemed that all of them were a bit fed up with where they were in their lives, and during one of our evenings in the pub we were discussing a German guy who had been deported from the UK, owing a fortune in tax and who had built a business employing students selling paintings on velvet door to door.

It was like another of those light bulb moments. As I sat I thought about if we could find a similar product and by using the same selling method develop our own business. This could help us change our lives, and for me it could get me away from a job I really hated, and also find a better place to live. After our discussion my friends and I were all of a similar mind and as the enthusiasm built we decided we would go on journey of discovery and hunt for this product we could sell.

Over the next week or so we visited loads of wholesalers looking for this elusive product, then one day we stumbled on some imported oil paintings that were produced in a cottage industry in Belgium and only cost £2.50 each wholesale, and so the 4 of us, Graham, Geoff, Roger, and myself bought 6 different paintings each and set out to test the market on a big new housing estate some miles away, to see how they would sell.

Filled with enthusiasm and posing as art students, within a few hours we had each sold around 4 paintings, with everyone quadrupling their initial outlay. After our first successful night, we reinvested all the money into buying our initial stock, and so the journey began to a new future and it wasn't long before I was earning three times what I was earning at the tank factory.

Everybody was elated, and we went out selling virtually every day for the next few weeks building up a good stock level, as we ploughed every penny back into the business so we could all put our pasts behind us and start this new fresh adventure.

The business grew and grew and we started to employ more and more people to sell for us, so much so, we rented a shop as our base so we had somewhere to store all our stock. I gave up my other job after 3 weeks, and as the shop came with 4 bedroom living accommodation, we all moved in together and everything was again looking up.

We all became really good friends, and went to many live concerts or clubs together, the business was booming and life just got a whole lot better.

We regularly placed advertisements in the local newspaper advertising for student types to sell for us, and the only time any of the four of us went out selling ourselves was when we felt like it as we were employing up to 30 people daily. We also repainted the shop, and started selling from it using it like a gallery, and in doing so the income from the local passing trade was enough to pay the rent. One day, a very attractive young lady called Michelle and her friend Sue walked into the shop responding to our adverts and looking for a job. It would be very wrong of me to say anything but it was 'love at first sight'. I was instantly totally smitten, and of course, they were instantly hired.

Michelle was very beautiful, with long blonde curly hair and beautiful blue eyes. She was very well spoken, was very bubbly and looked about 18 although I was later to find out she was actually only 15.

I gave her my personal attention and ensured she was in the team I took out each night, and eventually, after a couple of weeks, I plucked up the courage to ask her out to a live concert which she accepted. I remember it was a Pink Floyd concert at the Free Trade Hall in the centre of Manchester, which was an incredible concert. As she watched the band, I watched her. I couldn't take my eyes off her, as I was just so smitten by her, thinking all the time, "how lucky was I?"

Life just seemed to be getting better and better all the time. It felt yet again that everything just kept turning up at the right time, as if somebody was bringing everything into my life as I needed it, forces at work I couldn't understand at this time, but a feeling I was getting very used to acknowledging.

That said, things just got stranger as one day I was out driving locally and a car came out of a side road and hit me full on in the side, at high speed. My car rolled over 3 times and it actually ended up with my car upside down on somebody's doorstep.

As they opened their front door to see what had happened, I got out of the car through the driver's window with nothing more than a scratch on the back of my hand, when in fact I should have been killed instantly as the car was a total write off and the roof was flat to the driver's seat. I was shaken up badly for a few days but felt really lucky to still be alive, and bewildered how I got out of such a bad crash with just a scratch, and I had to ask the question again, had I been protected by my angels again? I was unable to find another feasible answer.

Having recovered after a lot of pampering from Michelle and a lot of persuading from my other friends, two weeks later to the day, I got back behind the wheel of another car and I decided to go visit Irene and the girls.

On my way back home I was again driving on a main road and lo and behold yet another car came out from a side road, hit me full on the side and sent me rolling over again, until I eventually came to a halt, crumpled up against a big public red phone box. This time, I wasn't aware how many times I rolled over, but it was several times. Instead this time, I was aware of my life flashing before me, but coupled with this feeling, there was this enormous sense that I will survive this, as if somebody was saying to me "Don't worry you will be fine" and I heard it clear as day, so I didn't panic at all. Once again, the car was a write off and I crawled out through the window and ran immediately over to the other car, to check if they were alright.

In the car, I found a guy in the driving seat, and his heavily pregnant wife in the passenger seat, although pretty shook up they were both fine, so I looked upwards and said thank you for protecting us all. He was so full of apologies, as he knew it was his fault and said "I just lost concentration for a moment". Then as he looked through his broken windscreen, he looked at my car and asked me how on Earth had I got out of the car in one piece? In fact, up to him asking that I hadn't even thought of myself, and looking at the state of the car I was pretty surprised myself.

With him saying that it spurred me into spending a few minutes looking at my whole body from top to bottom and in amazement finding once again I only had a scratch, but this time it was on my arm and I had ripped my shirt, and I mean it was just a scratch, and with very little bleeding.

To survive one total write off car crash in the way I did was unbelievable, but to survive two similar crashes was nothing short of a heaven sent miracle. If I was ever to need proof of Guardian Angels or guides protecting me, I had just been given it.

It took me a couple of months to get back behind a wheel again as my confidence in other drivers had been shattered, and I remember thinking to myself, "what next?", what was awaiting round the next corner? What new experience are you going to throw at me next? But even now, I realised that I had grown to be very accepting of everything that was put in my path, as I had learnt and was convinced that something or somebody was protecting me every step of the way.

My relationship with Michelle grew, and I started to love her deeply, but because of our age difference and especially because she was a month or so short of 16, although she looked a lot older, we had kept the physical side of our relationship on hold.

On her 16th birthday, Michelle asked me if I would pick her up and drive her somewhere, which I agreed to. It turned out to be a sexual advice clinic - she had arranged an appointment with the intention of going on the contraceptive pill so that our relationship could take its next natural progressive step. Although it was her birthday, I felt like all my birthdays had come at once - this virgin male was finally to become a man, be in a real, loving, complete and physical relationship, and I fell deeply in love with her, and our relationship blossomed, and was wonderful.

After around a year or so, the business started to slowly go downhill, as money in the country was getting tight, and the sales started dropping dramatically, so much so we had to let go of most of the people that worked for us, retaining just a handful to keep things ticking over and paying the rent.

In order to keep money flowing in we also decided to do a food tent at a local 3 day music festival in a place called Bickershaw up in Lancashire selling hot bacon and sausage sandwiches and burgers. It rained the whole 3 days and it was thoroughly miserable stomping round in the mud. As miserable as it was, we made a few hundred pounds profit and got to see all the bands for free.

Things went from bad to worse as we were also hit with the miners strikes, and massive power cuts in the UK, which went on for weeks. At the same time my ex-drummer, Graham, from the group I had in the army, also finished his service, and so I invited him to come live and work with us so that he did not have to go through the same experience

I had coming out of the army, making his transition back into civilian life a lot easier.

The minors strikes went on, and the power cuts became worse, and the business just came to a grinding full stop, as most of our business was done at night the power cuts made that impossible, so something had to be done and quickly.

Just going off at a tangent, we were living in the 70's, and most young people including my friends and myself were occasionally smoking marijuana and listening to music for recreation. It was the era of peace, love, and Bob Dylan, and going to live music gigs was the most popular recreation when you could afford it, so it was a very free and unrestricted sort of time in this period, and all young people were doing it. I suppose I've told you that so that you understand, I was just a normal young person of that time, and certainly not perfect, and just human like everybody else.

One night, while listening to music, we decided that the best thing we could possibly try selling at that moment with all the power cuts, would be candles, as they were in short supply in the UK at that moment.

So convinced were we about this plan, that we hired a 3 ton truck, took out all our money from the bank and headed over to Belgium to purchase as many candles as we could fit in the vehicle, hoping to make a massive profit, and it would only be a 3 day round trip.

The idea, up to this moment we thought was great, however, on the ferry coming back home 2 days later our plan went up in smoke as we listened to the evening news, only to discover that the miners' strike was being called off, and power supplies would be returned to normal.

Devastated would be an understatement of how we felt. We now had a 3 ton truck full of unwanted wax and had spent everything we had.

In the end we did actually sell the candles for around half of what we paid for them and so we could at least eat and pay the rent for a few months. Had the strikes and power cuts gone on for just another 48 hours we would have doubled our money as people were waiting for us to return and buy what we had.

We were now back to square one, Graham, Geoff, and Roger decided to move back home, leaving just me and Graham my drummer friend, in the shop and a new idea and plan of action was again urgently needed to keep us afloat.

One night, again whilst listening to music, my friend Graham said, "why don't we open a club like the roundhouse in London we used to go to?" Graham and I loved all the live bands and the atmosphere of the Roundhouse and the place was always packed to the rafters. Manchester however, had nothing like it at that time and considering Manchester had the largest student population in Europe it was crying out for such a club.

We discussed it all night, looking at what it might cost and how we would do it, but the only problem we could see was that we had no money, which was a pretty important missing link. During our time selling paintings we had come across many business people with money and so decided to re-contact some of them and try and influence them into backing us. So we racked our brains to think of who we could approach and made a list. I was never short of what they call "the gift of the gab", and some people said

I could sell ice cream to Eskimos, so filled with enthusiasm for this new venture we set out to try and find the funding.

We managed very quickly to arrange several meetings with people we had come across, and it only took a couple of weeks before we found someone, who knew a guy in London, who might be interested in putting up the necessary funding to get the project off the ground, so we arranged a meeting with him. We explained the project, and how much we thought it would take to get it started and off the ground, and from then on it would be self funding. He was very interested, and our backer, who we will call Mr M, said he had some disposable funds that he could make available very quickly, however, he didn't want anything on paper that traced back to him.

So we struck a gentleman's agreement about repayment and off we went in search of the perfect building. We didn't bother too much about where the money was coming from as long as we got the show on the road.

After a week or so of driving around Manchester, we actually stumbled on a building not far from where I grew up as a child, which had been first of all a cinema and then a cabaret club but was now closed down. It took us a couple of days to track down the owner, and we were able to strike a rental deal from him.

We gathered all our friends, stripped and repainted the building, applied for the Licence, struck a deal with a brewery, contacted various agencies to pre-book some bands for the opening night and week, had posters made, and finally everything was put in place. We decided to call the club "Stoned Ground" as it was going to be a rock venue. However, after police's objections we dropped the "d" and made it one word "STONEGROUND". Even to this day there are a couple of web sites on the internet created by past fans of the club who really loved it. Again I don't want this to be about the club, so I will just say it was an incredible time and the club became a piece of the North of England music history showcasing 5 bands a night, 5 nights of the week to an audience of around 1500 people a night.

My relationship with Michelle was wonderful, she loved the club and I often took her with me to London to meet agents and book bands and generally have some fun.

I got immense pleasure and satisfaction from running the club knowing that all these people were having a great time because of something I did, sort of like a public service, bringing happiness and Joy through music.

Graham, Michelle, and I moved to a rented house and over time we took in a couple of people we came across in the club who needed a helping hand.

We all became good friends, and I especially got close to one of the guys we took in who was called Paul, and he became the closest to a brother I ever had. Although he had lots of personal problems, he was a lovely guy and I helped him resolve some of his issues and get over them. We had a very special connection and I was able to read him like a book. Some days it was so strong it was like I could read his every thought. So much so, on occasions it scared him and he used to say it was like I was inside his head looking round.

I personally believe that this was the real awakening of my psychic and Empathic abilities which I think was triggered in some way, through the earlier car crashes.

At around the same time, I also started being able to read all sorts of people in the same way, picking up all their emotions and it was like a light switch had been flicked on, and a new world opened up to me.

We had another guy called Tony come and live with us who had arrived at the club as part of a road crew for a band, and he just wanted to stay up North, and not return to London, so we welcomed him into our family. He was a really nice guy, had a heart of gold, and fitted in so well and we became good friends. After around 40 years apart, we have somehow got back in contact, and today he is a member of my page, and is still the same kind hearted guy I knew back then. To me, taking people in and giving them a helping hand was just repaying some Karma for those people who had shown me some similar kindness. After around 2 years of running the club, I was called to a meeting with the guy who had originally financed us, only to be told even though he had received most of his money back, that he was going to bring some guy up from London to take over the running of the club and told me to surrender the licence over to this new guy. He went on to say that I could carry on working there, but neither Graham nor I would have any responsibility for the running of the club. Because there was nothing on paper we couldn't really do anything legally, and it wasn't as clear cut as that, and I can hear you saying, how could I let him do that after all the work we had put in.

You have to understand that this guy who backed us had big connections to the London gangster world, and in fact the guy he was bringing up to take over had run a club in London where the UK's most notorious gangland people used to hang out.

He was not a man to mince his words, and he let me know in no uncertain terms that the alternative to not doing as he said could have severe consequences for my health, and that is putting it lightly.

Being a person who was opposed to violence of any form, I decided to back out gracefully, and with dignity, and so I surrendered the licence and declined to work there, although my friend Graham stayed on and moved out of our house and in with his girlfriend. Me and Graham never met or communicated again after that point and I learnt after some time that he eventually moved to Canada with his girlfriend to go and work in his brother's hotel.

Now my life was to move to another path yet again, and more change.

However, there was some satisfaction gained in the knowledge that the club failed and closed within twelve months, maybe it was some kind of Karmic repayment for what they did. Who knows? I did various jobs over the following months, in fact anything that brought in some money including waiting on and bar work, I even worked in the packing department of a company owned by a friend of my girlfriend's family for a while.

One day, my girlfriend Michelle said that horrible sentence, "I think we need to talk", and she started to discuss with me that she had been offered a job in a seaside resort, down in the south of England, and felt she needed to get away, and discover who she was, and what she wanted from life. Because she had been with me from the age of 15, she felt that there was so much she had not discovered about herself or the World, and although she loved me dearly she just had to do it. She also went on to say that she didn't want any kind of long distance relationship because she needed total freedom, and that a clean break would be best for both of us.

I was totally heartbroken and we both cried for ages, but I had to agree that she needed to go discover herself and the world, and told her that I would never forget what she had brought to my life and she would always have a special place in my heart. Probably the hardest relationship decision I have ever had to face in my life.

We could call this another awakening about human life.

For me, having to understand that voluntary sacrifice is sometimes necessary even when you love somebody so deeply, was a hard lesson to learn. It is the realisation that we cannot selfishly hold somebody back when they have the need to experience and expand, the very purpose we are here living this human life. So, with a very heavy heart, and many tears, we parted. Another chapter was to close, and another new chapter was to begin, such is the natural flow of life, but she will always be my first love, hold a very special place in my heart and memories, and I will never forget her and the beautiful time we had together.

After a few months, I got back into the routine of life and going out again, yet not looking for anything in particular to happen. On one Saturday night out at a local rock disco with some friends, I was attracted to beautiful, long red haired girl, probably the first girl I had seriously looked at since splitting with Michelle. I was so drawn, in fact, that I plucked up the courage to ask her out, even though I remember being very nervous at asking, and then very relieved when she said yes.

Her name was Martha, and we saw each other virtually every day for around 6 months. She restored my faith in relationship, and we had some wonderful fun times together.

We became very close and the relationship seemed to be blossoming day by day and we fell in love.

One day, she came round quite distressed, and I asked her what was wrong.

She promptly told me that she was pregnant even though we had taken precautions, but as I was so attracted to her it took no effort or thought for me to say I would marry her, and take care of them both. She was very relieved at me saying that, and so we arranged to meet her parents to tell them together. Things definitely didn't go the way we thought it might. Her father went ballistic and said if I went anywhere near his daughter again he would see I regretted it. I didn't take this as an idle threat, as the family were very staunch Irish Catholic and I was fully aware of the dislike at that time between Catholics and protestants in Ireland. He also told me that she would be sent to Ireland to her aunties, and that I would never see her again, and that is exactly what he did. There was no reasoning with him. He just wouldn't listen, and so yet again, I lost somebody very special in my life.

I couldn't understand his hatred of me being an English Protestant, What had religion got to do with anything? Why is religion the source of so much hatred in this world? It is something I will always struggle with, but he made it very clear where he stood and ordered me out of the house.

To this day, I've never seen her again, but I did bump into her sister one day, some months later, who told me that whilst in Ireland, her sister had gone through a miscarriage. I still don't know if that was truthful, or what she had been told to tell me by her father should she ever bump into me. If it is not true, somewhere out there could be a child of mine, who I've never known, and who never knew me, and probably never will because it would have never been told the truth about its father.

It feels very strange, writing this, my life story, reliving all these events and experiences, and although I have gained a great human understanding from all I have gone through up to this point in my story, I had also gained many spiritual understandings that would serve me well along the way. All these experiences enable me to be empathic, and understand so many real situations when others seek my help and guidance, because I can speak from experience. It has been like a big preparation for something to come further down the road.

And so the story continues, and new paths were to be put before me.

In Retrospect

I have found writing my story very enlightening around my own personal development, and how and when life has put me firmly in contact with my higher self, with all these individual awakenings helping to create the person I am today. I actually recommend writing down your life story to anybody, because if you get nothing else from it, the experience will help you purge so much all the emotions and attachments you have to your past. Meditation can help you examine what is going on in your life now, but looking at your whole life is so different.

In this section of my life, I met my first true love, but from that love I had to learn about self sacrifice, I learnt that it is always possible to love again, if you keep your heart open to it, and also the need at times to put the needs of others before my own.

They say everybody you meet in your life is for a purpose, however, we don't always see it at that point in time. Michelle taught me how to love, and what it feels like to be loved.

But I also learnt how not to be selfish, how to put the needs of others before yourself and that people will pass in and out of your life. No matter how painful your experience might be life does not end there, it continues to flow.

We have to reflect that life must go on and that these human experiences are just like a season. They come and they go. They are not a life sentence to carry around forever. They are all merely lessons to make you stronger. I often hear stories of Near Death Experiences, where people die and then return and their whole life changes because of their new enlightened understanding that we are connected directly to your source. My own experiences around the car crashes is that although I never died in either of them it was just not my time to leave this life for some reason, and I got to feel the power of heaven and the Universe directing my life and protecting me.

I can look back now, and the only way I can describe how I felt as both crashes were happening, was as if I was in some big protective bubble and no matter how crumpled the cars got, I would be safe. In fact I realise looking back, that my life, it has been led in a fearless way, and living this way has enabled my life to keep flowing in the knowing that I will eventually reach the place the universe has planned for me. I now have a firm belief that when my time actually comes, I will know it is time. That little voice will tell me my mission is complete, and I will just accept it, also with no fear. Acceptance has played a major role in my life, every situation that I have gone through I have just accepted as part of my path, part of my learning, and therefore never feared change and never let fear energy hold me back.

I have also witnessed how divine timing comes into play. If something appears at the wrong time or the wrong place something will happen to change that timing.

"If there Needed to be Proof"

After everything that had happened I felt that I had yet again been thrown back into the human wilderness, and was floundering trying to find reasons and a purpose. It was like trying to find a pathway home when you find yourself in the middle of a deep dark forest at night and haven't a clue which direction to go, yet looking for that glimpse of light that would lead you out.

Even though I was already acknowledging on a regular basis that something or somebody was guiding my life and protecting me, and always putting opportunities in my way when things were going wrong, I still had some apprehension about what might happen next. What was in store? Where was it all leading me to? When will I discover the purpose? Yes I had seen the light but had no clue where it was leading me.

Then once again and totally out of the blue, like a bolt of lightning striking my brain, I had this sudden inspiration of becoming a male nurse, where it came from I am really not sure, it was that little voice again. Like many thoughts that had gone before, it was like somebody whispering in my head saying this is next for you. So, having been fed this thought and trusting my intuition, the next day I went along to my nearby training hospital which was only a short walk away from where I was currently living, and got all the information. At the meeting with a clinical tutor I was informed that because I had no formal school qualifications, I would have to take an entrance exam to determine if I had the aptitude for being a state registered nurse or a state enrolled nurse. The difference between the two was, that becoming a state registered nurse there would be a pathway to promotion, but a state enrolled nurse didn't have that pathway.

The other difference was that one entailed a 2 year training course, and the other was a 3 year more in depth training, plus of course a big difference in pay.

A week later, I took the entrance exam which I passed with flying colours, and was accepted to start training as a state enrolled nurse in a few weeks' time, as part of the new intake of student nurses. Being a training hospital part of being accepted was that for at least the first year you had to live in the hospital accommodation. So I informed everybody back at the house that I would be moving out but would be able to meet up with them on a regular basis as the hospital was only a short walk away. Upon starting the course I was surprised to find that I was the only male in a class of 32, plus I was also the oldest member of this new intake of nurses. This had its good points but also some very embarrassing moments, especially when learning male anatomy and being used by the teacher as a model which was hilarious for all the girls, but very embarrassing for me. One male teacher even made me stand at the front of the class with my arms out outstretched and said "this is a Uterus pointing to my body and then pointing to my arms said these are my fallopian tubes" I can't begin to describe how embarrassed I felt, being referred to as a part of female anatomy, and yes all the girls laughed out loud. Life was good, and once again I was back on my feet moving life forward, and it felt so right to be doing this new job, caring for people. There was always this underlying thought running through my head of why have I now been given this to do, why this job? Where does this piece fit in my life's puzzle? It was like so many questions I had asked my guides, but yet again, no answer was forthcoming, just a feeling, a knowing and understanding that there would be a purpose.

During training, we had to do 6 weeks in school covering theory, followed by 6 weeks practical experience on the wards and going on a different type of ward with each rotation, so we covered male and female, medical and surgical, children, burns unit, psychiatric, just about every area you could nurse in, and when in school we covered a different subject matter or area each time.

Living in the nurses' home certainly had its advantages, with the main one being a very short walk to work each day. I really loved the job, and it was great fun, as there were only 12 male nurses and over 200 young female nurses living in the nurses' home.

For most of the young nurses, they were living away from home for the first time in their lives, and were out to have fun as well as develop a career, and it was virtually party time every night in the nurses' accommodation.

I sailed through my first years training with ease yet began to realise very quickly that although I loved this job more than anything I had ever done, I was becoming a little too empathic with the patients, as I started to come out in sympathy with all the symptoms of their illnesses. Although I understood and was aware that these symptoms were not real, it was still troubling me, and I couldn't stop it happening. After discussion with one of the ward sisters she informed me that this was not uncommon especially in new nurses, but I needed to learn to control it or it would get worse and result in me actually being ill myself. During the second year of training and although I had dated many of the nurses on odd nights out, I became very serious with one young nurse in particular, called Rose. She was small, had blonde hair, very beautiful blue eyes, and was of Ukrainian background.

We dated regularly and when we were not going out, and I would either spend the evening in her room, or she would stay in mine watching television. The relationship grew very fast and became so serious that after 6 months we got engaged to be married. I remember constantly searching for reasons behind the paths my life had gone down, and remember thinking that I had been given the experience of living within a large group of men whilst in the army, and learning all about male behaviour, and now I was living with a large group of females and learning everything about female behaviour, so my guides were showing me both sides of the coin and the differences.

One day after work, she came to my room with a face like thunder and bluntly announced that she was pregnant, even though we had been taking precautions.

Although it came like a thunderbolt out of the blue and I was totally shocked, because we were already engaged

I saw no problem in just bringing everything forward. In fact, I was quite excited about it all as I always wanted to be a father.

However, my bubble was soon to be burst, as it became very clear that she didn't feel the same way. She told me that she was going to have a termination, as she wanted to finish her nurse training because it was so important to her, and that she wouldn't change her mind. In fact she had known for some days about her pregnancy, but had kept it to herself while she thought about it. I have to admit that I really struggled getting my head around her decision, and I was devastated, I couldn't understand how she could possibly think like that, how she could put her career before a child? Needless to say, this brought the relationship to a very abrupt and difficult end, as abortion was contrary to my beliefs.

I have the belief that if my mother had taken that view, I wouldn't even be here, but instead she gave me life, no matter how difficult her situation may have been, so I am very anti abortion, unless it's in the interest of either the mother or babies health.

It took some months to get over the relationship and the loss of my child, and it was very difficult to make any sense of it all. Even on a spiritual basis, I struggled, and just had to accept in the end that it was about divine timing, and the time wasn't right for whatever reason.

As both Rose and I worked in the same hospital, bumping into each other would occur, so we went out of our way to avoid each other. Neither of us mentioned the pregnancy to anybody, so that we didn't become the talk of the hospital, and when asked why we split up, we would say it just wasn't working between us.

I just got on with everyday life and threw myself into my work and study to distract me and be able to put behind me.

What was to happen next was to be the most awakening spiritual experience of my life, something I never expected and something I would never be able to forget.

I was on night duty on a male medical ward, and had gone for my dinner break as usual at around midnight. I was half way through my meal in the staff canteen when I heard this voice in my head, telling me I needed to go back to the ward, which I couldn't for the life of me, understand why this thought had been given to me, but not being one to ignore my intuition (that little voice in my head) I headed back to the ward. Upon arriving back I noticed a lot of panic and commotion going on in a side ward, and so I went in to see what was going on.

As I looked in the side ward, and to my astonishment, the cardiac arrest team were there working frantically on my dearest friend Paul, trying desperately to resuscitate him, which they finally achieved after a couple of minutes.

Within 15 minutes, he had another heart attack and so the team brought him back again, and at this point I hadn't even had the chance to find out why he was there in the first place. He did however look very yellow and terribly poorly, and was unconscious and not aware of what was going on. Some 10 minutes later he had a third and final heart attack, but this time the crash team failed to bring him back.

They called time of death, and the crash team left. I stood there all alone with tears rolling down my face for the loss of my dear friend, my self- adopted brother. All of a sudden the whole atmosphere and temperature of the room changed, and I can only describe it as peacefulness that came over the room. As I looked at Paul's body, I felt this calmness, and what I can only describe as a thin veil, or mist, with no shape or form rose from his body, hovered above him for a second or two, and then disappeared upwards and out of sight.

I cannot be sure what I saw, I cannot explain the atmosphere and emotion of that moment, but I personally believe that I saw Pauls spirit leave his body. I can't find any other explanation for what I saw and felt, unless the shock caused me to hallucinate in some way. My personal belief is that this was the whole reason behind me becoming a nurse in the first place, so that I could have this heavenly experience. Divine timing, right place, right time, the final proof shown me if I needed it. As I look back on this, I can even relive all the emotion and feeling of that moment, and the total peace and love that filled the atmosphere.

Part of a nurses job is to lay the dead out, ready for transfer to the morgue, but I was so disturbed by what I had just gone through that I phoned the evening matron on duty, and explained that I had just watched my friend die, and could I be excused off duty, because I couldn't face being there, which she instantly allowed without hesitation, and arranged for another nurse to cover my shift from another ward. Early the following morning, there was a knock at my room door and it was the nurse's home sister who said she had been informed of what had happened the night before, and I was advised that I had been given a week's leave from duty to recover.

I actually went to the ward later that day to discover what Paul had died of, only to be told he died of blood poisoning, caused through drug use and that all his organs had failed. In fact, I was later to discover from friends that somebody close to him had sold him some drugs that were cut or mixed with something bad, and it was that which had caused his death. So much for friends! Around a week later, I attended Paul's funeral and all through the service I felt his presence, as if he had come to watch his own funeral and see who was attending.

I even had the vision, of him just standing there peacefully smiling at me. Was this my imagination, or wishful thinking, or was he really there saying his goodbyes?

In my mind it was the later. All I know is that I left the cemetery with a feeling that he will always be around me, and strangely enough, I have always felt his presence around me since that day. Just recently, I don't have that feeling, and in my thoughts I have a knowing that he is now content in the knowledge that I have found my spiritual path, and so I don't need him anymore, but I can call him if I do.

I went back on duty the following week and carried on as normal not telling a soul what I had seen in case they thought I had lost my mind, but even to this day I can recall what I saw the night he died vividly and smile when I think of it.

As I got into my third year of training I moved out of the nurse's home and got a flat share nearby, with another couple of nurses, and back in the hospital I formed a relationship with another of the nurses. We spent most of our time when off work together, and even though I no longer lived in the nurses home myself, I spent most nights in her room in the nurse's home and we became really close friends. She had discussed with me that she didn't like nursing, and regretted joining but couldn't leave because her parents would be disappointed. I at the same time, was now having serious problems dealing with the empathic side of me, and seemed to be developing every illness under the sun, and it was getting worse, I had already decided to leave nursing altogether. It was always a very strange feeling, knowing on one hand these symptoms and feelings were not real, but on the other hand still experiencing them, but that is empathy working at its best.

One night during a conversation, we both decided that it might be a good idea to get married, then she would have a reason to give up nursing without disappointing her parents, and on my part, I'd find something new and maybe look forward to fatherhood as I'd always wanted to have children, and so it seemed a great solution for both of us even though we weren't what you would call passionately in love. She was my dearest and closest friend, and I suppose we thought love would just come in time if we were married, maybe naive yes, but I know it is how we thought at that time.

We went together to tell her parents, and being a bit of a traditionalist, I asked her father for his permission. Although her father was fine about it, her mother showed some disappointment at her giving up nursing, but my girlfriend agreed that she would just take a year out, then go back into nursing, so they both accepted it, and we went to buy an engagement ring. I left nursing after I served a month's notice and got a job firstly as a shoe shop trainee manager and then as a branch manager. I remember that in just about every branch I went to, that there was always some elderly member of staff that wanted to mother me, not sure what it was about me that sent out that signal, but it became a common occurrence.

I left this employment to become a salesman for a kitchen company that gave me an opportunity to earn more money. It turned out as you will see that this was to become a good move for me around developing my future.

As if I hadn't already been shown a lot of protection and guidance, here comes another little story about how the guides create situations and how the law of attraction can work.

We hadn't got enough money to put down as a deposit on a house and so were looking for somewhere to rent, prior to our marriage. One day I was looking at the newspaper at work, and got to the back pages where all the details of the days horse racing could be found. Now, I wasn't a gambling man at all, I had never placed a bet in my life on anything, but I had this incredible powerful urge to place a bet on the racing of that day. In fact, I understood so little about placing bets that I had to ask a colleague to explain to me how to do it, and so he showed me all the different ways you could place a bet.

One of the ways was what he called an accumulator which I liked the sound of. It meant that I had to pick 6 horses and this would then include doubles, trebles and so on, and the total bet would cost £16, which was a lot of money back then, in fact around half a day's pay. But I just knew I had to do this. It was that little voice in my head again, and the feeling of being pushed to do it regardless of any human thought. So I placed the bet, and we sat in the shop and listened to each race on the radio, and I couldn't believe what was happening as each of my horses won, until eventually the last horse went passed the winning post in first place, and I very quickly went back to the betting shop to find out how much I had won.

To my amazement I had won just under £1600 and because it was a Monday, and they hadn't taken enough money, I would have to come back the next day to be paid. This amount was just enough to put down as a deposit on a small cottage we had seen, so once again my angels and guides had provided just enough that was needed.

Shortly after leaving nursing, and just before getting married I was drawn inexplicably to start going to a local spiritualist church, something I had never done before and I think the purpose was to try and find some answers and understanding for my life's journey, and all these experiences that had happened to me.

After I had been going there some time, I met some wonderful people who went out of their way to explain things to me, including the late great British medium Doris Stokes, who I was very drawn to. She was the first person I heard say, "We are not humans having a spiritual experience, we are spirit having a human experience" something all modern spiritualists throw in nowadays, as if it's the first time it's ever been said, but I first heard this 40 years ago.

Many from the church took me under their wings and were all keen to answer my questions, and they then invited me to join a psychic development circle, which they advised would help me, and so my new spiritual journey was to commence. Hopefully I would be able to find a little more understanding.

Around the same time I started visiting spiritual fairs, which I found fascinating. I loved the atmosphere and eventually had a couple of readings done as well as listening to many lectures.

My first ever reading was done by an old lady in her 80's, who was a very gentle peaceful soul who you felt very at ease with. It was quite a spooky, yet very accurate reading, and she wasn't a card reader. She was a medium who just sat there voicing all she picked up. Yes, I had watched some stage mediums perform, and it was quite often very vague from where I was observing. This was a new experience being one on one and felt quite different.

She told me I was surrounded with music, and asked if I had been linked to music and big white building? This of course, was my rock club, and it was a big white building. She told me I would be married and would have three children, and she also saw a lot of travel around my work and moving house several times, she also told me that there was a very special purpose behind my life but couldn't elaborate on that. At another fair I sat in front of this older lady who was actually responsible for organising the fair to have a reading done. She was not in good health and carried an oxygen tank and mask around with her. As I sat in front of her she just blurted out, "why are you asking me for a reading? You should be this side of the table. You have the gift".

I was a bit taken back, to say the least, and asked with curiosity what she meant? The reply came, "You will become a better reader than me, you just need the right teacher." I laughed, and said, where do I find this miracle teacher? Her reply was short and brief! "I'm sat in front of you".

I had to laugh, I suppose because I thought she was just touting for business teaching Tarot. I went on to explain to her that I was soon to be married, and couldn't afford to pay for somebody to teach me, to which she replied "Who said anything about payment, I will willingly teach you as long as you are prepared to learn and work hard, and maybe you could repay me by doing some of my fairs later down the line".

It seemed a good deal to me, and so a week later, we arranged for my first lesson which I found very difficult to understand, but we persisted, and it started to sink in. We very quickly went to around two lessons a week for almost a year, which varied each week with a different day or time convenient for both of us.

I was working, so it was fine for me in the evenings, and she had many clients she read for at her home during the daytime, so it worked well for both of us. She was a hard teacher, often swearing at me to go deeper inside me, trust my feelings, trust my intuition, say what I saw and felt, and our lessons went on until at around 70/80 lessons later, she thought I was ready to actually do a readings on my own.

I can always hear her saying her favourite line as we pulled a card, "Look at the card, and tell me a story, tell me what you see, think, and feel", and this is exactly how I teach nowadays following her example, and many of my students love the story telling way I also teach.

I kept my promise and appeared at her psychic fair, and I actually ended up doing many of them, so much so I built up quite a following of regulars, and eventually doing many private parties from my attendance at the fairs, which I really enjoyed doing as we also had lots of laughs.

During this same year, I was sitting in my psychic development circle, every Saturday morning at the spiritualist church, and I could see my connection getting stronger every time I did it, and I attended the circle for around 10 months in total.

I occasionally went to the Thursday night services to watch guest mediums if I wasn't working late, and at one of these such nights, I had another incredible and out of the blue experience, again something that would stand out in my life as being another very big spiritual moment and awakening of my psychic abilities.

After the guest medium had finished doing their bit at each service, they would always ask the audience if anybody would like to share anything they had been given for somebody else in the audience, and this was common practice.

I had rarely seen anybody actually partake in this way, but during the mediums performance, something kept drawing me towards a middle aged woman in the audience, and each time I looked at her I was getting this strange unexplainable image. So, when the medium asked the audience I raised my hand, stood up very nervously and said "Yes, I have something, I've been shown to give to the lady over there in the red coat, I know this sounds very strange, but I feel the need to give you a bottle of HP sauce for some reason" well, as soon as I said it the woman broke down in tears, and in a very tearful state said thank you so much.

As the service was wrapped up, I was very eager to talk to her, but I didn't have to wait, as she came over to me, and told me that her husband had died only a few weeks earlier, and that he put HP sauce on every meal, no matter what it was, and so she took this as a message from him that he was safe and fine. For me, the experience was strange, and I remember saying to myself, did I really just do that?

It was very much a reinforcement for me that I was now firmly on my spiritual path, and all these things that were happening were for a reason, although I had no idea what that reason or purpose would be.

My girlfriend and I got married, and we moved away to this little cottage in the countryside, and she got pregnant within 3 months of being married, which ensured she wouldn't have to keep her promise to go back to nursing, but unfortunately her father died of pancreatic cancer a couple of months before our first child was born, so he never got to see him.

After her father's death, we moved house to a nearby town, and was in the middle of renovating it when the kitchen company I was working for had grown massively, and I was asked to move to the South of England, to help open and run a new office in London. The offer was very lucrative, financially, and after discussing it with my wife, we took the offer up and moved south. In the south we had a big house, very good life style and income, and we had our second child, a little girl. I worked long hours and sometimes six and half days a week, as we were a direct sales organisation and I had around 150 salesmen on the road. I was commuting around 100 miles a day to and from work, so my working week was long and hard, some days leaving home at around 7am, and only returning home at around 9.30pm.

Even though we had a good life and my wife wanted for nothing, she became very home sick, and wanted to move back home as soon as possible. So we put the house on the market, and I arranged a transfer back to head office in Manchester.

I loved my job in the South, and it was doing incredibly well and so I was very sad to be leaving, but to keep harmony in the marriage, I went along with the move. You need to understand that although our marriage seemed perfect on the outside, to anybody looking in, it wasn't a marriage based on love and passion. It was based on a mutual understanding and just friendship. At the start, we were very close friends and I think we thought that love would come in time, but the cracks were already starting to show, and love was just not going to happen. I worked hard, and gave her all I could, and I have to admit, she loved shopping, but that was never going to be enough, as the love needed to hold a marriage together was missing.

Things didn't work out very well back at head office, even though I was given a titled executive position, decent salary to go with it, and a nice Mercedes car. I missed the daily thrust of being at the front end of the business, and all the guys I worked with, but my wife was happier being in the familiar surroundings of her home town and some friends she knew, and so I stuck it out, even though I was unhappy. Eventually, I was headhunted by a rival kitchen company to go and work for them, which I only took up because I was offered a directorship and shares in the company after a year's service. Unfortunately, when the time came to be given the directorship and shares in the company, the owner reneged on his agreement, and so I walked away from the company. After this happened, I decided instead of building companies for other people why don't I do the same for me, build something solid for me.

And so I used all the money I had, and I set up my own kitchen showroom using every penny. I did very well for a year or two until all of a sudden Interest rates in the UK started to rise and rise rapidly until they reached 15%, the highest they had ever been, and which crippled most families.

The knock on effect was that business fell through the floor very quickly, as people stopped doing home improvements and I eventually reached the point of having to put myself into bankruptcy. The bankruptcy meant I was losing everything, my business, my home, literally everything I had. All I managed to keep was my car and some dignity as I put myself into bankruptcy rather than waiting for somebody to do it to me.

Before I put myself into bankruptcy, I moved the family to a rented house to ensure they had a roof over their heads, and give them some kind of security. Here we were yet again, having to adjust to another totally new lifestyle.

This was even more difficult for my wife, as she was used to having and spending money whenever she wanted, whereas money has never bothered me as long as I had enough to get me through, but now things would be very difficult, probably the hardest ever as I was effectively unemployed.

My wife was pregnant at the time of the bankruptcy and shortly after our move to the rented house, my third child was born, another son, which would make things even more financially difficult and put more pressure on our relationship.

In Retrospect

This period of my life was without doubt the most esoteric and eye opening part, with many things developing and being shown me.

Each experience encountered took me a little further along my spiritual path. It was like things were deliberately being shown me as proof. Divine timing was once again showing its hand, in that it was not the right time to become a father with Rose proving that either the time or person was all wrong.

That said, in the end I married not for love, but so that my children could be born, something I will never regret, as I love all my children. It is so surprising how things work out, and I have realised life is full of them.

My marriage was based on the wrong foundations, however, I served a purpose for my wife, and my wife served a purpose for me, and so I recognise that this meeting was arranged, and meant to be in divine timing, and for a divine purpose, the main one being my children had to be born.

It was also the right time to take up the things that I would need later in my life, the tools that would open doors and set me firmly on the last part of my spiritual journey. Even to this day, I am amazed at the divine planning that has gone on in my life, so that everything was prepared and ready for the right time and place, and then it will come to the fore, and serve as a guiding light for others. Over and over throughout my life my angels and guides have arranged for me to be in the right place at the right time, with the right people appearing, people who I would learn from and would guide me forward. How could I have possibly imagined at this time in learning to read Tarot that it would be something that would come in and out of my life, and then 40 years later re-emerge to be the catalyst that brings me to become a spiritual mentor. Even at the inception of my internet page 18 months ago, I had no idea of where teaching Tarot would take me, and that my spiritual beliefs would turn out to be the driving force behind everything I do.

I used the word Esoteric at the start of this retrospection, because what I experienced with Paul, at his death, esoteric is the only way I can describe it, for if we look at the dictionary meaning of esoteric it is described as "Intended for or likely to be understood by only a small number of people with a specialised knowledge or interest" So, for me, it was a spiritual vision sent and meant for me to confirm that I was on the right path, and that this path would be a spiritual one and this would reinforce my belief.

I actually feel very privileged to have had this experience, as it is not one that everybody gets to have, and actually it is something I have kept to myself from that moment until I told my life story to my twin flame. In fact, most of my life has been on a need to know basis, and even my ex wife doesn't know some things I have retold in this book, and my children, no none of it, except I had the club and the part they lived through. I am normally a very private person but I feel it is time to tell so that other people may learn from my experiences.

My Tarot teacher is one of only a handful of people I have met in my life that I could truly put my hand on my heart and say she was, without doubt a genuine true medium- vessel, who did what she did teaching me because of her calling. She had the knowing that she was supposed to teach me, and she did unselfishly, and with a passion like it was part of her purpose for me to be the best I could be, ready for the journey ahead. Like Divine timing putting everything in place ready for the right moment. I hope that what she taught me, I am able to pass on in the same way, and with the same understanding, passion, and love that she had.

Tarot will always be a part of my life no matter where my spirituality takes me.

"From All Endings Come New Beginnings"

During this period of unemployment, I did a lot of thinking, and one of the things that sprung to mind was to try and start searching for information about my birth and my parents, the roots from where I grew. I got the Salvation Army involved as they had a great record of 70% success rate of tracing people, I also wrote to the RAF, as my father according to my birth certificate was a serving corporal when I was born, additionally, I wrote to the children' services at the local council, who would have overseen my fostering. I went on all the genealogy sites to search their records, in fact, every angle I could think of and try, in the hope I could unearth something. It wasn't long before people started getting back to me; in fact the first to get back in touch was the local social services department, who informed me that unfortunately, all records were destroyed when a child reached 21, except for a basic index reference card. My index card showed that I was already living with my foster parents at the time that social services were contacted and got involved. Apparently from their records I was 10 months old when my foster parents contacted them, and I had been living with them already for 3 months, but that is all that was on the card, so no reason behind what happened, and how I came to be with them, and so the truth of the story will never be found as both my foster parents are now dead. This official record was totally contrary to what my foster parents had told me, and the story that I had been taken off my mother because she hit me was just a total lie. Yes, it leaves ne with many unanswered questions around the fact that my foster parents must have known my mother in order to take me in, as you don't just take in a stranger's child, and if they knew my mother who was she, how were they linked? So this first result got me no further, except to unearth the lie I had grown up with.

Next I received a reply from the RAF, who said that the service number listed on my birth certificate belonged to somebody who was killed in the 1914-18 war, which was at least 27 years before I was born, so either the number was written down wrong at the time of registration, or again it was another lie? In addition, they said that they couldn't do searches based on names, and so I hit another dead end there.

The genealogy sites also turned up nothing after weeks of trawling them, and so I turned to the government records office of Marriages, Deaths and Births which also turned up blank with absolutely no trace of any records relating to either of my parents. I even went through a period of roughly 20 years of records, 10 years either side of what I thought their rough ages would be.

So dead end after dead end, it was like I arrived from nowhere, and this made me realise that maybe all the information on my birth certificate was just a pack of lies. Just like I said at the beginning of this story, I felt like

Moses, abandoned and found floating in a river to be raised by strangers.

I suddenly had a flash of inspiration to try and track down my eldest foster sister, who was some 20 years older than me with the thought that she might know something, because she was already grown up at the time of my arrival into the family. So I set to work tracing her. Eventually, I tracked her down and arranged to go round to see her, which was quite a strange experience as I had not seen her for many years. I had the hope it would bring me a little closer to the truth. But it turned out that she didn't know much at all, but told me all she knew.

All she remembered was that before I was officially fostered, and at the age of around 9 months old, my father came to see me.

She remembered that he was in uniform, but from memory it wasn't a British uniform, and that he brought me an apple to eat, even though at that age I had no teeth, which would indicate to me he didn't know much about babies. Other than that, she remembers at some point she overheard a short conversation around a possible older brother my mother had given birth to before me, and that was it, everything she knew. So I ended up not really any wiser, except to know that my father obviously had some attachment to me, he probably wasn't English, and so maybe he had come to say his goodbyes?

Putting what I do know together, I look at my Mother's name, Phyllis Teresa, which is very Irish Catholic, also, I have two children with red hair, which would imply my mother was of Irish decent, which would explain no record of her birth in the UK records. My father from what my foster sister told me, I can presume was American as many USAF people were based in Manchester, especially in the district I was registered to at the time of my birth, and even his name, Perry would imply that, as it is a very American name, so again why I could find no records in the UK. After a year, the Salvation Army who are known as being the most successful tracers in the world, also came up with a total blank, and so I will never know the truth of my arrival into this world. Every birthday I religiously give thanks to my mother, wherever she is, for at least having me, and giving me the chance to have the incredible life I've had.

Back into the family situation, it really was a difficult time financially after going bankrupt, and I would do just about anything that came along to earn some money. I was really feeling at the lowest I had ever been, with a total loss of direction.

It had been 12 years since I had picked up my tarot deck or done any readings, but because of my situation, I remember thinking that maybe it's now the time to re connect, and so I placed a postcard advert in several of the local shops, and started almost immediately to get clients and so started doing home visits and parties again. It flowed back to me so easily and was like I had never been away from doing readings. I didn't want to get involved in psychic fairs again at this point as the one thing I didn't like about doing them, and from my earlier experiences, was running the gauntlet outside every fair of placard waving Christians outside each venue, saying we were working with the devil. These people had no idea or understanding of what we did, or our belief system, but they were out to condemn us because our beliefs were different to theirs.

I also started going back to the spiritualist church again on Thursday nights in order to reconnect with like- minded people and to watch the mediums practising their gifts with a thought that maybe one day I could be like them.

Sadly, many of the people I had met years before were very thin on the ground.

I soon got to know some of the new people who were really nice and made me feel very welcome and at home. I even went to a couple of spiritual fairs to discover all the previous nonsense that went on before with Christian protests had stopped, so I got back involved, doing several over the following months. I remember one of the fairs very clearly, where I had a queue of around five or six people sat there waiting for me to become free, and I was very drawn to a young woman in her mid twenties sat in the queue and each time I looked at her, I had these thoughts running through my head, and I would chuckle to myself as my intuition kicked in again.

When it was finally her turn, she sat in front of me and I told her what had come into my mind while she was waiting, I said," I know why your here, you're having an affair, and you want some guidance which guy to choose!". The moment I said it, her jaw hit the ground and she was in total shock saying "how do you know that?" I said, it just came to me as I looked at you, and this little voice spoke to me. It turned out she had only been married about 6 months and was in fact having a relationship with another man, and she had come seeking some guidance what to do, but the advice I gave her will always remain client confidentiality. It was personal proof that my intuition or psychic ability, call it what you may, was reawakening, but it certainly doesn't happen at will, or all the time, it comes and goes as and when it needs to.

The way this happens to me always makes me very suspicious about performing stage mediums that seem to be able to call up spirit at will, which is certainly not the way I find it happens. If spirit wants you for any reason they will contact you, not the other way round. I mean, it's not a telephone exchange; you can't just dial up a spirit.

I really needed something more concrete to do for a living as I was used to working long and hard and needed something that could provide a regular decent income.

As I had really loved nursing, even though it didn't love me as it made me ill because of my empathy, I decided to go back to college and take a qualification in social care management, which would enable me to be a manager in a care home, so old people not sick people.

I researched what was available at the local college, and found a course that fitted the bill exactly, and because I was officially unemployed, the course was free to attend, and I could still claim my unemployment benefit whilst doing it.

At the same time I started my course, I also started to volunteer at my local community centre after responding to their advert for help, and as my course was only part time, I could fit it in easily working what hours I had to spare. They were having financial difficulties and needed somebody with fresh ideas to help them get back on their feet.

Money was very tight, but somehow I managed to bring in enough to keep us going with the readings I was doing.

Again, as I looked back on my life at this point, I had this reaffirming realisation that no matter what had happened something, somehow, had always fallen into place and moved me on to the next thing, and in doing so, I always had just enough. Somebody and something unseen always seemed to be at work in my life, moving me forward, taking care of me, providing for me, and ensuring that I learnt many lessons along the way, in addition to the spiritual awakenings, and I just couldn't deny their existence.

We managed to get through the next 2 years while I was at college, and I eventually qualified on my course with honours, something I was very proud of, especially in my cap and gown at the presentation of my qualification.

I had also worked very hard to build the community centre back into a good financial position, through the introduction of many new services for the elderly, and into a position where they could actually afford to employ me full time, instead of me looking for another job, which I would have done because of my newly obtained qualification, the first qualification in my life. So things started to look up again and another journey was to start.

Just 12 months after joining the community centre full time, I also got involved in local politics, after being encouraged by people at the Centre, firstly on the local parish Council, and then I was asked to stand as a County councillor, and to my surprise, I got elected.

With the earnings from the community centre plus the county council, we were able to move out of the rented house and buy a local house, which although needed renovating, was still a bargain at the price we paid for it, and it gave me a feeling of recovery and re building my life once again.

Over a period of 18 months or so, I had repeatedly been getting bouts of infections, some of which made me quite poorly, yet I generally worked through them as I hated being away from work. I saw several consultants over a period of 2 years, and none could make a firm diagnosis, until eventually after seeing many of them, I was diagnosed with a failing kidney. Once diagnosed, it wasn't long before I ended up in hospital having a major kidney repair, and was told that afterwards I would need at least 8 to 10 weeks off work to recover.

Through positive thought, I was back behind my desk 10 days later. Although I was still a little sore, I was feeling fine and strong enough to just get stuck back in.

I was working some 70/80 hours a week, but all the work was very rewarding, not only financially but emotionally, it was very fulfilling.

At County hall, I became the champion for older people's services and also chairman of the committee that looked after children in care, amongst many roles, and I had made many friends and admirers through the work I was doing, and it was so rewarding, being very much involved in making people's lives better.

At the community centre, we won various national awards for the educational work we did with older people. We ran computer courses, language courses, art classes, craft classes, Yoga classes, and many more, all aimed at the over fifties, and getting them out of their homes and being active and not lonely. In total I had 36 different classes running, so something for everyone. We also had dance classes and evening entertainment, and which all contributed to making the Centre the real heart of the community. It seems my life was always to be one of service, in some way.

I also managed to raise over £1.5 million to build a modern, state-of-the-art education block at the back of this old building, that was originally built in 1830, as a village school, for miners children, an achievement I was very proud of, as I was making a difference to people's lives and providing something worthwhile for the community.

The only thing that was wrong in my life was my marriage, which had gone downhill, and we were growing further apart, doing our own things instead of together. My wife had no interest in the things I was involved in. I was a politician, and she hated politics, and the only thing she had any interest in at the Centre was her line dancing, and so because of our differences, I buried myself in my work to avoid any confrontation and facing the truth of my marital situation. By the time my youngest child was around 4 or 5, I was fully aware that my marriage was over and that we were just going through the motions, yet because of how I came into the world and grew up as a child, I just couldn't bring myself to deserting my children, and so vowed that I would stay and do nothing until my youngest was of secondary school age, so just grit my teeth and bare it.

I carried on working long and hard to avoid being at home. I even started dancing, doing modern jive to give me an excuse to not go home several evenings a week, and with my wife doing her line dancing, I suppose was to do the same. When I was at home, I started spending all that time being focused on the children, playing with them or taking them out, anything to avoid too much time around my wife, and this went on for around another 7/8 years.

Even on family holidays, I spent most of my time just entertaining the children in the swimming pool, or doing something with them while my wife just sunbathed. I knew the end was coming, and I'm sure she knew it as well. It sort of became the unspoken thing between us and we were two people living different lives, and the divide got bigger and bigger.

When in the same room we didn't have to speak to each other, but you could just feel the negative energy exchange and divide between us, and I'm sure the children felt it at times too, although they never said anything.

My eldest son moved out of the family home, and in with his girlfriend, and my daughter went off to the USA to work on a Disney cruise liner, so only my youngest remained at home. My youngest reached the age where he went up to senior school, and so I decided I couldn't go on like this anymore in this loveless marriage. I needed to find myself again, and I had kept the promise I made to myself, that I would stay until he reached this age. After he had settled into school for a couple of months, we had that dreaded conversation, the one that all married people dread having when their relationship ends and they finally have to face up to it, as hard as it is you know that it has to be done.

It was October and one night after some tiff over something very small, so small I can't even remember what it was. I just said "we need to talk as we can't go on like this with both of us being unhappy". We were both quite upset and shed some tears, but that was more to do with ending the familiarity of 28 years of marriage rather than the loss of a loving relationship. I said that I would stay for Christmas and then look for somewhere to live which my wife agreed to. It is the most difficult conversation you will ever have, when you recognise that you are in an empty marriage. It is not easy but is essential that you have it. You cannot stay in a marriage because of familiarity. You cannot stay in an empty marriage because you fear change, nor can you stay in a bad marriage because of children. There is in fact no reason to stay in a marriage that just destroys who you are. You are put on this Earth to live your life to the full, and it should bring you joy, not sadness. When we had had this discussion, so much tension was released, and even though we had arrived at a decision of how and when we should part, which would be after Christmas. It didn't work out that way in the end, as in the November a female friend I knew from my dance class at the community centre who knew about my marital problems, offered me a room in her home anytime I wanted it. As we were already good friends anyway, this seemed an easy way to move out and move on, and not prolonging the agony any longer, so I accepted and I went home and told my wife. Two days later I packed a bag and moved out and moved in with Sue and so that was the end of 28 years of marriage. It was a marriage that came about because of all the wrong reasons, not a marriage arrived at because of love, and yet somehow, it still lasted 28 years. The only regret I have about the marriage is that we should have ended it much sooner than we did.

I remember arriving at Sue's, and I just broke down in tears with this massive sense of relief that at last we had faced up to the truth, and let go. All those years of stress and anxiety that had built up at staying in a loveless marriage, and all that day to day negative energy could be released.

Sue hugged me for ages and consoled me, and I was so glad to have somebody there to deal with the emotional fallout.

During the following months, as I got back to being me, Sue and I became quite close, going out dancing on a regular basis, and we even went on holiday together to Minorca, and so developed this close relationship. It wasn't love by any means, it was just two close friends being there for each other, sharing a life, having fun, and without any ties. She was also divorced, and had two grown up children who lived away from home, and I met them at that first Christmas, and we got on well, so we were in similar situations and just enjoying each other's company.

The first year had its problems with my ex wife being a little difficult over access to me seeing my youngest son. Even though I continued to pay the mortgage on the home and support my son financially, she was still a little bitter, but eventually we resolved it, as my youngest son insisted on seeing me. He started visiting me at the community centre most days after school and things soon calmed down. Then we got to spend day's together going out or just being at my place. I can't say that me and my ex wife are now the best of friends, but at least there are no longer Ill feelings of any kind between us. My only ever fear about the separation and divorce was that my children would hate me, but in reality we became closer, and my youngest even came and spent weekends with me and Sue, who he really got on with and liked.

The next 18 months had its ups and downs. My wife was in a new relationship and moved the boyfriend in to the family home, which I was still paying for, so I stopped paying the mortgage and gave them the option of him buying my share, or selling the house and splitting the profit, although I would still be contributing for my young sons upkeep. After around 2 years of living with Sue, I had a massive fall out with some of the new people on the management committee of the community centre, who were totally disrespectful towards me, and so I walked out of my job after 16 years dedicated and loyal service to the community.

My term of office as a councillor also came to an end a few months later, after 8 years of service, which was also quite emotional because I loved the work I did there.

My divorce was eventually finalised, and my relationship with Sue came to a very abrupt end once I lost both jobs and became unemployed, I think she had a fear of having to support me which scared her so she asked me to leave, so I found an apartment and moved out within a week.

Quite a big emotional roller coaster during this time to go through, and now there I was having to live on my own for virtually the first time in my life, and it felt like life had thrown everything at me but the kitchen sink, and had brought me to yet another beginning, another new path to tread.

The first year on my own was very hard, and I struggled with it. It was very lonely, after being surrounded by so many people every day throughout my life. Things calmed down, and eventually I got used to my own company. Then one night out of boredom I started playing on line games and started meeting and chatting to people.

Over a couple of months, I really got to know a group of people from one game in particular. We became online friends and would discuss each other's lives on a daily basis, and which removed any loneliness I may have been feeling.

In Retrospect

Affirmation after affirmation happened during this time, and I was made fully aware that I had been gifted with being able to connect to the spirit world, not in the way you see stage mediums perform, but on an occasional basis, and with a specific purpose being behind it.

I still get goose bumps when I think of the woman in the red coat who I gave proof of her husband's continued existence, which I detailed in the last chapter, and still chuckle to myself as I revisit the look of horror on that young woman's face when I told her she was having an affair.

These were, however, personal confirmations of my connection to the spirit world as strange and mysterious as they were to me. I love doing Tarot readings and the way it connects me to other people's lives in strange and mysterious way.

I look at Tarot being far removed from fortune telling, as I am certainly not a fortune teller by any means. It is just a tool that enables me to get into somebody's life, and see where they are at, and then lets my intuition jump in to help guide them along their journey. I am a firm believer that nothing in life is set in stone, because we were gifted "Free will", that thing that separates us from the rest of the living world, and enables us to makes choices instead of reacting to instincts. Therefore, we can change paths anytime we wish, should we have enough courage to do so. Sometimes, the hardest bit is recognising what would serve us best.

Looking at my whole life up to this point, it feels like time after time I have been put here to serve other people, to bring them joy like I did, with my rock club, through music. Bring healing which I did through being a nurse. Bring them learning which I did through what I built at the community centre, or bring them protection and purpose which I did as a councillor.

Through everything I did, I was also to learn lessons along the way which were put in my path to make me a better and stronger Empath, and bring me wisdom and understanding of human life, so that I could go on to serve a much bigger community.

Another very strange thing that has happened over the years, is this ongoing feeling which has grown stronger with time, that everything has been to prepare me for something much more important but even at this point I have no idea what that is.

It is a feeling I can't explain. It is a feeling that just doesn't go away and is with me every day, and feels like all the lessons I have had to learn. All the experiences I have had to go through, were to place me firmly on my spiritual path, and this could just be the start of my real journey. Looking back over my life, I can't see anything left that I could possibly have to learn, or any experience I may have not had that would be necessary, but considering my life to this point and how things have just appeared in my life then nothing would surprise me.

I feel like I have been through spiritual primary school, secondary school and finally spiritual University, and I am now ready to head out on my spiritual career and wherever that may take me.

"A Return to where we Started"

As the title of this last chapter suggests, we will be arriving back to where we started, at the beginning of the book and the present, but there were still a couple of surprises to jump out at me. Once again, the pages of my life turned, and life was going to move on yet again, all heading me to my spiritual destination.

I was 62, and had to accept that I was at an age where nobody was going to employ me again, regardless of my knowledge or capability as we live in an ageist society.

I therefore had to just accept that this was some kind of forced retirement, from a normal busy working life and 3 years before official retirement age, hard but a reality.

I was also living on my own for the first time in my life, something else I was having to adjust to, but I made some really good friends through gaming online, and so all the initial loneliness I felt soon disappeared, as I had lots of people to talk to every day. I was so glad I had learnt how to increase my computer skills on one of my own courses at the community Centre, and I was so glad for the internet. I see these now as another essential preparation to enable me to move onto my final spiritual path, because without this knowledge I wouldn't be doing what I am doing now. It's all part of divine timing.

Life was yet to throw another curve ball in my direction, when in the spring 2015, I noticed a patch of skin in my groin turning quite peculiar and so went to the doctors. He instantly referred me to a consultant who immediately diagnosed skin cancer. Although it was a bit of a shock, like many things I had gone through in life, I just took the blow on the chin as yet another test of faith.

Rather than sit there getting all worked up, wallowing in self pity, and building up fear energy about the future, I asked for strength and guidance from my guides and angels, and asked that I remained positive, and that I could get through this like I had got through all the setbacks my life had thrown at me.

I was determined to beat this, and on my own, so much so, that I did not tell anybody that I was ill, except a couple of internet gaming friends, not even my children, as I didn't want them spending their lives worrying about me.

My thoughts were, that if I told them, they would just worry and fuss about me and that would be creating negative energy, which wouldn't help anything and also impact on their everyday lives, feeling they had some obligation towards looking after me.

We may be a spiritual being, but we always have to remember that we are existing as spirit within a human body, and human bodies fail and have an expiration date. The Earth and all living things upon it are prone to all sorts of diseases, and so many of us have to go through them, and because I am spiritual does not make me any different. I got through the many months of treatment and just carried on as if nothing was happening, and letting nobody know I was ill. I meditated a lot drawing down as much healing energy as I could, and focussed all my energy into fighting my own body, and staying positive that I would beat this. Only my doctor was aware of what I was going through, and I would put on a brave face when I saw my children or neighbours, as any form of pity would have not helped. Everybody would have made a fuss. When my treatment came to an end I was happy and relieved as the treatments side effects were probably far worse than the effects of the disease.

I could now start on the road to recovery in the hope that it was dealt with, and I could move on and get back to normal. Several months later, I was told that we had in fact caught it in time, and it was cured, although I would need regular checkups to ensure it didn't return. I eventually told my family and friends that I had been poorly, but I was now over it, and was declared cancer free and after their initial annoyance I hadn't told them, they were happy. The only downside was that unfortunately, because of the treatment my immune system was low and I developed several chest infections over the next few months, which knocked me a bit sideways, but again I ploughed through them with the use of antibiotics, and by the end of 2016, I was back to my normal healthy self.

I will never know if the power of positive thinking, or healing sent from my guides and the Universe had anything to do with my recovery, but again it was not my time to return home, that I can be sure of. Maybe just a human illness cured with human resources, who knows? Either way my positive thoughts are what got me through it giving me hope.

Other endings that happened at this time were that the divorce with my ex wife was finalised and she and the new man in her life arranged to buy out my share of our house, which I used to clear all the marital debts which were around £106,000, and so I had another clean slate that gave me great relief.

After paying off all the marital debts, all I had left from the sale of the house was enough to buy a decent second hand car, not much to show for 28 years marriage, but I had achieved everything I wanted from the marriage by having my 3 children and now have 3 beautiful grandchildren who I will always be grateful for.

I will never say my marriage was all for nothing. It gave me the greatest things I have in my life, my children. My eldest children are in good relationships and have children of their own and my youngest son has gone through University with flying colours, achieving a 2:1 history degree, and is now pursuing an acting career, much to the dismay and disappointment of his mother. Acting is the real love of his life, and he will be moving to London this week, to take up a place he was offered after beating 5000 applicants to a place at the most prestigious acting schools in the Country. I couldn't be more proud of him, and I am sure he will succeed in his chosen career, as he's already had some considerable success in acting and directing and because he has a thirst for life and a positive mind. I see so much of me in him. Although my children are fully aware of my spiritual beliefs, and that I read and teach Tarot, I have never tried to influence them with my beliefs and never do anything in front of them. I want them to just discover life for themselves, form their own belief system, and make all their own mistakes, so that they learn from them. So that is where everybody is at, from my past life up to this moment, except to tell you my wife remarried last year, and has moved away from our village. So, this now brings me back to where this story all began, with Kelsey getting me to start my own page and group through Tarot. You have shared with me a journey through my life, with all its ups and downs and contrasts, and everything that brought me to my spirituality now, a long journey. You have been able to join me in all the many spiritual awakenings, big and small, that have placed me firmly on my current spiritual path, even though at this point, I still have no idea where it will be taking me next. All I know is that all my lessons have provided me with a great understanding of human life, and it has helped me support many people through their journey.

In Retrospect

I can sit and look at everything I have gone through as lessons I had to learn in order to be the Empath and spiritual mentor I am today, and as they say "been there, done that, got the T shirt" well, my wardrobe is bursting with T shirts, both human and spiritual.

I know there are still more experiences waiting out there to happen both human and spiritual, but I am at that stage where nothing will surprise me anymore.

At this point, even though I consider myself fully awake spiritually, there is so much I still haven't experienced, plus I have still not been given the final details of the rest of my journey and the purpose for it, so I will wait in anticipation.

Writing my life story has enabled me to purge the last of any emotions or any attachments I had left from the life I have lived so far. It has cleansed me and enabled me to totally let go of everything. I hope that anybody who gets to read this story, that they will be able to gain something from it, no matter how small, and if nothing else, that they will learn that life is always meant to flow, so let it do what it is designed to do, plus that every experience you have is just that, a learning experience, a lesson put in your way to learn from. Everything that has happened on my life's path is as if my guides and angels have pushed me along it, guiding, teaching, and protecting me as I go though it took me a while to recognise what was happening at first. They have been very clever at creating all the lessons as my life moved along so that I covered so many aspects of human life that I would never have encountered otherwise, and in retrospect, I have absolutely no regrets about any of it.

I had no option but to learn, so that eventually I would be ready for whatever my life purpose was. Those lessons were hard at times, but hard was essential for my spiritual understanding of human life, and to ensure I learnt them.

I believe that even in writing this story, somewhere there is a purpose created by my guides and angels, and why they got me to write it in the first place.

One thing has just come to mind as I told you at the beginning, that I have never read a whole book in my life. Well, I can now put that behind me to, although I never thought the first and only book I would ever read from cover to cover would be my own.

It seems everything but the kitchen sink has been thrown in my path during this lifetime, human situation's many people would never experience or have to encounter. Alongside these human experiences come several spiritual experiences that have shown me the existence of spirit in our human world, a proof not everybody receives.

Everything that has happened has solidified my belief in the spirit world, plus, I have had many highs and great adventures along the way. But yet, I still feel that there is more to come, and I have not yet achieved the purpose for which I was sent here.

Even when I write articles for my page, I take the view that if I only help one person in their spiritual understanding, it is job done, and so hopefully writing this book will follow suit, and at least one person will learn or benefit from it.

The very last, yet important thing I need you to know about my life story, is that I have forgiven everybody in this story for their part in it, but most importantly, I have also forgiven myself for my part in any of the situations.

I have gained immense personal strength from my journey, and have learnt how not to build fear energy around making changes, because changes are what make our life flow, plus to recognise when the situations in your life no longer serve you. Change them, and if you can't change them, then let them go and move on.

Life and the Universe has a wonderful way of surprising you when you least expect it, so just let life unfold as it is supposed to do. Do not be afraid to let your life flow in whatever direction it wishes, as that direction has been chosen for a reason and chosen for you.

Always remember no human is perfect. We are not meant to be perfect, because if we were, there would no reason to be here and no lessons to learn.

You are allowed to fail, failure is natural and there is no disgrace in it, because through failure you learn lessons that make you stronger and wiser. So ensure you learn the lesson first time, so that it doesn't have to repeat itself until you do. It will make your life easier in the end.

I acknowledge without any doubt the existence of Earth angels, who have at times been put in my path when I needed them the most. They have taken me away from difficult situations, picked me up, showed me compassion and understanding, along with giving me direction, enabling me to get back on my feet and back on my path. Although I may never find the truth behind my birth, I will always give thanks to my parents whoever they are, and wherever they are, for giving me my physical body in which my spirit could live. Without you, I wouldn't exist. Finally, to the Universe, I would like to say thank you for giving me the chance to experience so much, so that I could expand my spiritual being and understanding of this human life.

Whatever Heaven and the Universe have planned for the future, I will go with a willing heart, and be the best I can be, so that I can shine my light and give love to the world before I return home. Bring It On, I am ready and waiting.

As the purpose of this book was to show my life of awakenings, and how I reached my consciousness and spirituality, I also think it would be remiss of me to not talk about, or comment on, how I have observed the changes within spirituality and the spiritual community over the same lifetime, as a conclusion.

These comments are just a personal opinion on what I have observed.

When I started getting involved within the spiritual community over 40 years ago, it really was a different world, Spiritualists were totally condemned by the Christian community as being people that worked with the devil, and I witnessed many demonstrations outside spiritual meeting places by these Christian groups.

During my earlier years, you were a spiritualist on a need to know basis. You kept your beliefs to yourself, and spiritualist churches, which were quite often just rooms in a building, not churches as you would think, were the only places you would talk about spiritualism, and mix with like-minded people, and feel at ease.

The very first person I remember being a public stage medium was the late great Doris Stokes who developed a massive following in the UK, but also had a wealth of critics, who condemned her as a fraud and a phoney. It was not only Christian's.

Having met her at that time, I can only say that she was one of the most authentic spiritualist mediums I have ever met, and she possessed a strong, loving energy about her that was infectious and warm, somebody to trust to guide you, but again that is my personal opinion.

Actually coming across another spiritualist in those days was a rare event outside of the meeting places, because I think people were just scared to admit their beliefs to anyone. This was for fear of verbal abuse, or repercussions by their Christian friends, plus there was also just a fear from people of something they didn't understand, thinking it was Hokus Pokus or messing with black magic, so little was their understanding.

As the years have moved on, things have changed so much. No longer do we have the demonstrations outside psychic fairs or spiritual churches by Christian groups. They are now just accepted as everyday functions by people with their own beliefs, plus many of these fairs now often fly under the banner of Wellbeing fairs, and encompass many things so a change for the better.

However, in some countries being a member of the spiritualist movement is still frowned upon, especially by what are called "Born again Christians", with anything spiritual being referred to as being against God and the Bible. We could argue all day about Spirituality versus Christianity or any other Religion come to that, but my answer to that is that "all roads lead to the same source", no matter what we call that source, and the only difference is how we travel that road. There is room on this Earth for everybody's belief systems without condemning those of opposing views.

It is just a case of live and let live and acknowledging the connectedness between all living humans.

The arrival of the Internet with all its wealth of information at your fingertips has been the main contributor to the massive expansion of the spiritual community, and those now following this path from every corner of the globe.

Thousands of video's, pages, groups, and written pieces can be found at the click of a button no matter which Country you may be in, and those searching for support, answers, knowledge, understanding, or just a place to belong, now have this wealth of information at hand, something that was just not available in my day, and so spiritualism was very much compact and local.

But, like everything in this world there are always two sides to the coin, a light and a dark, and the internet is no different.

Along with, and amongst all the genuine spiritual people and sites on the Internet, we can also find unscrupulous people, who have seen an opportunity to earn a living by scamming and preying on some of the most vulnerable people out there who are just searching for support and answers in their moments of need or distress. This totally infuriates me when I see many examples of people doing this. I see on a regular basis people charging ridiculous fees for all kinds of spiritual courses, and offering worthless certificates upon completion, giving false hope to people. I too teach Tarot on the internet, to my own followers, but I charge a very modest fee, plus I am always there to support them and answer their questions, not just a faceless money making machine, and I will not give a certificate under any circumstances. Even though I have 40 years' experience, who am I to say that somebody is a qualified reader or not, and give them a certificate as some kind proof? The only person that can ever give that opinion and confirmation are the people who my students read for, and how accurate their readings are. The clients are the only ones that can give you that validation, not some worthless piece of paper that says you have completed some course. Where did these people who give out these certificates get their qualification from?

Most of what I do is totally free, and want it available to those most in need, those who need support and guidance in their time of need, not just to the few who can afford to pay. I am known for being straight talking, and I tell things as I see them after examining everything closely, even if it goes against conventional teachings.

My other pet hate at the moment is around misleading information being given out, giving the impression that everything in life comes easy, and it just falls from the sky, with the Law of Attraction being the main culprit. Don't think for one minute that I don't believe in the Law of Attraction because I do. It's the inaccurate interpretation of it being taught that I don't hold with, and it is misleading people to think it is something it is not. The part that I am in full alignment with, is that we attract things into our lives that are vibrationally in alignment with our thinking, so everything is linked to the thoughts you are having, and the resulting vibration you give out to the Universe. I am a great believer in energy being the source of everything, plus vibration and alignment being the link of what we bring into our life. What we think is what we attract, what we think affects our energy field, and therefore changes the vibration of our being and can attract like a magnet. If we are thinking positive thoughts we will attract positive results, but you can't expect to attract positive outcomes if you are a negative thinking person. In fact, the rules around the Law of attraction are very simple, not complicated at all. However, the myth that seems to be growing from everything I read or see in videos lately, is that if we just think of something we want, and then keep those thoughts going, whatever we are concentrating on and giving our energy to will just fall from the sky like some miracle, like a Law of Attraction delivery service.

If what is being preached by many at this moment around the Law of Attraction were realistic, and all we have to do is wish for it, then the whole world would collapse and be in turmoil in a very short time.

Everybody on the face of the Earth would have more money than they could ever need. Nobody in the world would be homeless or hungry. We would all have perfect loving partners. Nobody would work. Farmers wouldn't grow crops or raise animals to feed us. There would be no builders, no politicians, or law enforcement, no doctors or surgeons, as nobody would have a need or desire to work, so the world would just come to a standstill. Nobody would possess drive or enthusiasm for advancement, because there would be no need for it if you have everything just by wishing and thinking.

I do not come out with airy fairy explanations and mislead people, spiritualism is a reality to me, not some silly fantasy or some esoteric rubbish. There is an old saying that goes "Heaven helps those who helps themselves" and that is how I see Law of Attraction working. It would be a ridiculous state of affairs and totally unrealistic for everybody to have everything they want in life, nothing would have any value anymore, ambition and drive would go out of the window. There would be nothing to strive or aim for and there would be no lessons in life to learn. If everybody had everything just by asking for it, where would be the worth in this human existence? Where would be its point? I personally see law of Attraction as being like a two way contract, yes, the universe will bring things in your direction that are aligned with your thoughts and vibration, however, you have to perform your side of the contract and work towards that goal. You have to put in time and effort, and you will be given help and guidance in your work towards attaining it.

Failure to complete your side of the contract and be ready and deserving will result in failure of reaching your goal, things just do not drop from the sky.

So in conclusion, yes, spirituality has grown and become more acceptable, which I am very happy to see, and I get great joy from seeing the world becoming more connected and loving through spirituality.

However, the internet is a breeding ground for those people not so loving, so please move forward in your understanding and knowledge of spirituality, but be discerning and careful in whom you trust, especially on the internet. I will always remain nothing more than just another human, struggling through this human experience, learning my lessons as I go, and trying to make sense of our reason for being here.

I am just spirit having a human experience, and so even with all I have gone through in this life, and everything that has been thrown in my path, I love this world, love this life, and am grateful for my journey. Hopefully, I can enjoy this world a little longer, so that I may continue to spread my light. May your guides be with you, and guide and protect you, just as mine have throughout my journey.

Printed in Great Britain
by Amazon

77912880R00082